MW00824996

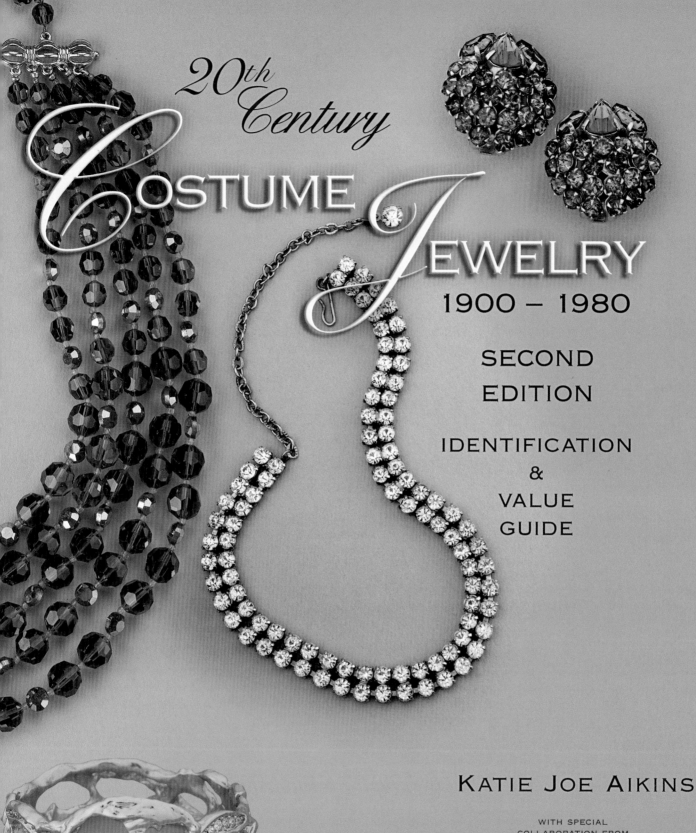

20th Century
Costume Jewelry
1900 – 1980

SECOND EDITION

IDENTIFICATION
&
VALUE
GUIDE

KATIE JOE AIKINS

WITH SPECIAL
COLLABORATION FROM
RONNA LEE AIKINS

COLLECTOR BOOKS
A Division of Schroeder Publishing Co., Inc.

On the front cover: Green and gold beaded necklace, $130.00 – 180.00. Rhinestone double strand choker, $45.00 – 65.00. Gold and black flower pin, $35.00 – 55.00. Gold and purple necklace, $135.00 – 175.00. Gold-tone vine style bracelet, $95.00 – 135.00. Pink and smoky gray rhinestone earrings, $150.00 – 180.00.

On the back cover: Lion necklace and clip earring set, $130.00 – 170.00. Beaded necklace and earring set, $95.00 – 135.00. Page 2: Goldtone and black lacquer necklace, $70.00 – 110.00. Purple and black flower pin, $20.00 – 40.00.

Cover design: Beth Summers

Book design: Lisa Henderson

Cover photography: Charles R. Lynch

COLLECTOR BOOKS
P.O. Box 3009
Paducah, Kentucky 42002–3009
www.collectorbooks.com
Copyright © 2008 Katie Joe Aikins and Ronna Lee Aikins
Updated values 2010.

All rights reserved. No part of this book may be reproduced, stored in any retrieval system, or transmitted in any form, or by any means including but not limited to electronic, mechanical, photocopy, recording, or otherwise, without the written consent of the authors or publisher.

The current values in this book should be used only as a guide. They are not intended to set prices, which vary from one section of the country to another. Auction prices as well as dealer prices vary greatly and are affected by condition as well as demand. Neither the authors nor the publisher assumes responsibility for any losses that might be incurred as a result of consulting this guide.

Searching for a Publisher?

We are always looking for people knowledgeable within their fields. If you feel that there is a real need for a book on your collectible subject and have a large comprehensive collection, contact Collector Books.

Printed in China.

Contents

Dedication

To my Papa, for the many times that he was sure that there might be two people in the world that are right, and he is sure he is one of them — and he thinks I might be the other. Thank you for your support, encouragement, and never-ending confidence in the areas of life that give me anxiety. Without you and your reassurance, the ER would have a chronic consumer in me. Above and beyond preventing mini-(impending) heart attacks, thank you for making a better person of me by your steadfast love and genuine example. Thank you for being the best Papa (and confidant) a girl could ever dream into life. I love you.

And to Geoff, because you're the end of my rainbow, my pot of gold; you're my darling Geoffles, to have and to hold; you're my sugar and spice and everything nice, and I love you. Thank God for mistaken identities and "whatever that was." Here's to our future as newlyweds and ever after....

Papa

Geoff and Katie

Geoff

Acknowledgments

Gail Ashburn, Amy Sullivan, and Beth Summers at Collector Books have been very kind and patient with me. They are so cooperative and easygoing. I also thank Collector Books for giving me an opportunity to not only enjoy a great hobby, but to document it and to share it with others.

From Ronna: Thanks to Whitey Aikins, my husband. This year was a real challenge; I really don't know how you fit the photography in your schedule, but I sincerely thank you. To Abbey Little, my niece, who is becoming interested in her aunt's jewelry collection. I think Abbey has quite the eye. At age 12, she has her pick of great pieces. Thanks to Quinn Little, my nephew, for all of his help packing jewelry.

From Katie: Thank you to my mom, Ronna, for being a patient helper. Thanks to Geoff for encouragement. Thanks to Mimi and Papa for all the laughs. Thank you to my friends at Homer-Center for always inquiring about my interests. You ladies are the best. Thanks to Kari Hain and Justine Rowles for lending ears. Julia, my dear friend, costume jewelry is just another one of our interests that we shared in a close friendship.

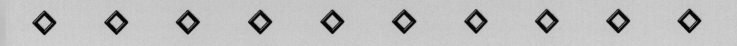

About the Author

Katie Aikins has helped her mom (Ronna Lee Aikins) with writing books since the publication of *Brilliant Rhinestones* in 2003. Katie graduated from Indiana University of Pennsylvania (IUP) in December 2007, with a master's degree in the art of teaching English. Katie maintained a GPA of 4.0 throughout graduate school. Katie graduated from Seton Hill University with a bachelor of arts in English literature in May 2006.

Katie never stopped sharing her love for vintage purses and costume jewelry. Katie frequently wore the jewelry and carried the handbags to school, which helped to introduce a new generation to the appreciation of the art, design, collecting, wearing, and shopping for pieces of vintage jewelry or spectacular vintage purses.

Katie has appeared in *Country Living* magazine with Ronna in an article about vintage costume jewelry. Katie has been in *Pittsburgh Magazine*, as well, in an article with Ronna about vintage handbags. Katie authored an article for *Small Town Life* magazine ("The Artful Dodger") about Ronna and Ronna's collection of jewelry. Katie is continually growing her collection of costume jewelry. Katie's admiration for the craftsmanship, art, and history of the jewelry allows her to continue to gain and seek more knowledge.

Katie and Ronna are often seen shopping the shows for the next unfound treasure. Katie's hobbies are reading, swimming, and shopping for her collection.

Katie

Note from Ronna

I would like to thank each of you who have purchased my books. I am elated to be surrounded by so many people who have the same passion for vintage jewelry. Due to *20th Century Costume Jewelry* being so well received, I thought it would be appropriate to offer a second edition with the same scope of styles and types of jewelry. Any adoring collectors that may have missed selections in the first book *Brilliant Rhinestones* or the second *20th Century Costume Jewelry 1900 – 1980* will find that the love for collecting just gets more intense. Still today I am truly amazed when I purchase jewelry that people can part with such a personal part of one's self or family — whatever the situation may be. It makes me question why family members don't hold onto their belongings. I hope my daughter, Katie, keeps my jewelry and purses that we have collected throughout the years. Katie will always have her memories of our collecting. She had better never give up my family photographs, now there is nothing worse than seeing pictures at antique marts!

Again, thank you and keep the driven spirit while collecting. Buy what you like and enjoy.

Values and prices reflected in this book are determined from the selling prices in the co-ops, antique shops, shows, flea markets, and auctions. Prices differ geographically. Price is also based on condition, quality, documentation, and designer of the piece.

Costume jewelry's popularity still soars. With the current state of the economy, jewelry prices remain strong for the defined and better jewelry. Today's women are wearing beads and chains in multiple layers. No matter what is in style, it is always true a piece of jewelry will dress up any choice of clothing.

Ronna

Care of Costume Jewelry

- Do not spray perfume or oils on your jewelry.

- If you store jewelry in plastic bags, this will enable the jewelry to resist moisture. Wrap loosely and store in boxes, drawers, or plastic containers. If displayed in an open area, cover with a soft cloth that will not catch the prongs.

- Do not place the jewelry close together. This can shift the prongs and loosen the stones.

- Like glassware, extreme heat and cold creates damage. Changing environments may also affect the jewelry.

- When storing earrings, place them on earring holders, if possible. If not, lay them flat. Bracelets and necklaces should be flat with stones turned upward.

- Do not place the jewelry in water. If water is between the stone and backing, it can tarnish the stone. Gently clean with a Q-tip and glass cleaner, watching that the prongs do not catch. Depending on the piece, you may want to use dishwashing soap. Then use a jeweler's cloth or a soft cloth to polish.

- Remove jewelry before sports, swimming in salt water, etc.

- Use a jeweler's cloth to buff.

- Store in an area that is not damp. Weather can ruin the finish, and extreme heat or cold can loosen the stones.

Displaying Jewelry

- Daring to display your jewelry shows just how creative you can be. This is where you can enjoy and have fun with your collection.

- Mirrors can do wonders for costume jewelry. Get creative.

- Frames provide a unique showcase for your collection.

- Glass top coffee tables are a nice way to highlight your beauties.

- Hang on windows so they can catch the light.

- If you have any mounts, display your pieces as it can be a fun way to show your prized possessions.

- Jewelry can be pinned to, or hung on, pillows, dolls, stuffed animals, and lamp shades.

Getting the Most Wear from Your Jewelry

Pins

- Give your clutch, evening bag, or hat a new updated look by adding a pin or brooch.
- Scatter pins over headbands, belts, jackets, scarves, and ties for a dazzling addition.
- Place pins over buttons on coats or jackets.
- Place a pin or brooch at the neck of a double strand of pearls.

Bracelets

- Stack them! Not only is this attention getting, but also a great conversation starter.

Chains

- Wrap long chains to create a belt or choker.
- Wear many in different sizes and lengths together.
- Do not be afraid to mix and match golds and silvers.

Popular Shapes

Round brilliant is the most popular and traditional.

Emerald is rectangular in shape, with facets on all sides and across the corners.

Heart is the most romantic shape.

Marquise is long and pointed at both ends.

Oval is patterned after the round brilliant-cut, and appears larger than the round stone with the same carat weight.

Pear is a variation of the round brilliant-cut and is pointed at one end.

Tapered baguettes are a popular choice for accent or side stones.

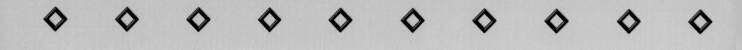

Birthstones and Meanings

January
Garnet: Promotes sincerity. Faith, friendship, and truth.

February
Amethyst: Is associated with royalty. Symbolizes confidence, strength, and wisdom.

March
Aquamarine: The gemstone that preserves youth and health. Symbolizes peace and tranquility.

April
Diamond: Worldwide symbol of love. Universally treasured.

May
Emerald: Unchanging faithfulness and love come to the wearer of this stone. Symbolizes growth and fertility.

June
Alexandrite: Sign of royalty. Named after Alexander the First of Russia.

July
Ruby: Associated with beauty, friendship, love, and passion. Symbolizes happiness and good fortune.

August
Peridot: From the Arabic word for gem or the French word for unclear. Symbolizes warmth and charity.

September
Sapphire: Known for durability and brilliance. Symbolizes faith, goodness, and truth.

October
Rose Zircon/Opal: Symbolizes beauty, inspiration, and serenity.

November
Topaz/Citrine: Symbolizes integrity and truth.

December
Blue Topaz or Blue Zircon: Said to have healing powers. Symbolizes strength and intelligence.

Company Histories, Information, and Designers

AVON: Designers through the years:
Seymour Kent, 1976 – 1980.
Louis Feraud, 1984.
Trifari, 1986 designed and made the 1986 Centennial jewelry.
Kenneth J. Lane, 1986 to the present.
Celia Sebiri for Avon, 1987.
José and Maria Barrera for Avon, 1989 – 1996.
Shaill Jhevari for Avon, 1993 – 1994.
Elizabeth Taylor, 1993 – 1997.
Coreen Simpson, 1994 – 1998.
Billy D. Williams for Avon Undeniable set, marked.

BOGOFF: Bogoff and Jewels by Bogoff usually were made in small quantities. High quality costume jewelry.

CINER: Originally made fine jewelry, and then in 1931, it began to produce high-end costume jewelry. Ciner used quality stones and faux pearls that were made from coated glass beads with a polished pearl luster.

COVENTRY: November 1949, started with home fashion shows and conducted business in that manner until 1984. A Chicago company bought Coventry in 1984, and began to produce jewelry for a Canadian company using the same name. Sara Coventry purchased designs that were manufactured by other producers of costume jewelry.

CORO: Coro jewelry was marketed under many names. Coro was the largest of all costume jewelry manufacturers. Corocraft was the higher end line. Later, Vendome usurped Corocraft to assume the "top of the line status." In 1979, after 80 years of business, Coro closed.

EISENBERG: In 1914, Eisenberg started as a dress company. Sparkling rhinestone clips adorned the dresses. The clips' popularity led the company to a new marketing strategy of selling individual dress clips. The clips were a huge hit! In the 1930s, it began to market jewelry. In 1958, it became a jewelry manufacturer exclusivly, and the clothing line was discontinued. From 1930 to 1945, Eisenberg Original Clips were produced. In the 1940s, E script was used along with EISENBERG ICE (most were rhodium plated). EISENBERG with block letters started in the 1970s.

FLORENZA: In 1950, Florenza started producing its own jewelry. However, it was in operation until approximately 1937, or the late 1930s under the name Dan Kasoff, Inc. In 1981, Florenza closed.

HOBE: Hobe was in business from the late 1800s to the early to the mid 1990s. It produced museum quality jewelry, yet it really was costume.

KRAMER: Was a leader in the production of fine costume jewelry. It used the best quality of rhinestones. Its earliest jewelry is highly sought after by seasoned collectors.

LISNER: Is noted for the colorful rhinestones and aurora borealis that it used to produce jewelry. The jewelry it produced was rated A- to B+, which means very good to great! The first mark, from 1935, was "D. Lisner & Co. in New York" in both block and script; marks also included "Lisner & Richelieu"; "Lisner" block, 1935; "Lisner" script, 1938; and a block type letter with a long L, 1959. These marks were used over a period of 55 years. In the 1950s, they produced a high quantity of jewelry. They offered a lesser priced variety of jewelry that sold on cardstock.

HASKELL, MIRIAM: She was known for handmade jewelry, careful wiring, and elaborate filigree offering a variety of designs. The filigree was usually electroplated goldtone with an antique finish. Before WWII, most of the crystals used were from Bohemia, and the beads were from France and Italy. In the late 1940s, the jewelry was marked "Miriam Haskell" on the hook or clasp. In 1990, the company was sold.

MONET: Known for high quality costume jewelry manufacturing. Founded by Jay and Michael Chernow. They began making jewelry in 1929. In 1937, the mark "Monet" was first used.

NAPIER-BLISS PRODUCTION: The company began in 1910. James Napier was the head of the company from 1920 to 1960. The company was sold in the 1980s to Victoria Creations.

TRIFARI: Trifari is known for the CROWN above the T trademark, and quality. In 1930, Alfred Phillipe came on as the head designer. In 1941, he introduced the Crown pin. Trifari's success led it to be the second largest company (Coro was the largest).

WEISS: Albert Weiss's 1940s company discontinued business in 1971. Some of its jewelry was purchased from the Hollywood Jewelry Company, and the Weiss name was applied to it. Its volume was not that of Trifari or Coro, but it had a good line of jewelry. Albert Weiss was highly regarded as a top quality designer.

Personalizing Jewelry

This vignette will help to determine what type of jewelry one should wear according to face shape, complexion, eye color, and hair shade.

First, let's determine your face shape. The four shapes are square, round, oblong, and heart.

A square face is straight with a squared forehead. The cheekbones and jawline are the same width; the jaw is the dominant feature. You look your best if you select a necklace that is in the shape of a "V." Wear round shapes at the throat that will soften the square jawline. Chokers with a circle design are also a fine accent for you. I suggest that you choose oval and round brooches, pins, and earrings. Rounded and soft-edged pieces complement you.

A round face is as wide as it is long with a short chin, soft rounded jawline, and hairline. You look your best if you select long lengths in necklaces or necklaces that end in the shape of a "V." Wear shapes that cause the eye to move vertically. These would be angular or geometric, which are square or diamond. You should choose dangle earrings in an angular design; pieces that add length will flatter you.

A narrow jaw with an angular chin and shallow temple with a high forehead make an oblong face. You look your best if you select oval or round beads or chain-link necklaces. Wear circular or swirl designs which will add width to your eye area. I suggest that you choose short necklaces or chokers to reduce the length of the face. Horizontal pieces add width to your face. This makes for quite a stunning accent!

The heart-shaped face has a prominent cheekbone. The face is wide at the temple and forehead with a tapered narrow chin and jawline. You look your best if you select round and square beads. Wear earrings that are wider at the bottom. Dangles and hoops complement you, too. Pieces adding width to the chin line give you elegance.

Suggestions to complement your skin tone, eye coloring, and hair coloring:

Dark and olive complexions look livelier in bronze-toned metals.
Pale complexions become vibrant with red jewelry.
Tan complexions are bronzed with whites in earrings, necklaces, and bracelets.
Warm complexions are glowing in golds, bronzes, coppers, and lighter colored rhinestones.

Hair:

Blondes should have fun wearing gold, coral, and pearls.
Brunettes do best with pearls, silver, burgundy, and garnets.
Gray is gorgeous with silver and platinum.
Auburn is amazing with amber, tiger's-eye, and gold.

Eyes:

Blue is becoming with aquamarines, lapis, and sapphires.
Brown is bright with tiger's-eye, amber, topaz, and amethyst.
Green is grand with emeralds, hazel tones, and jade.

What's Hot in Today's Fashion World

Women have always worn vintage jewelry, costume jewelry, and the real bling. The fashions of time influence the accessories and jewelry we wear, as does our age and economic and social status. Today, we are seeing a lot of the heavy gold chains, crosses, big, bulky significant necklaces (perhaps this stems from a fascination with popular culture or just the recycling of looks throughout the ages); bulky gold-tone bracelets, and pearls (a return to simpler times? A fascination with all things elegant? Or is it just the fact that the pearl is truly timeless?).

Today, popular pieces garner their designs from the early 1970s to the early 1980s eras. In the mid to late 1970s, gold was very popular. Remember the television show *The A-Team*? Mr. T. was decked in gold jewels. Present trends are also coming from the jewelry boxes of our mothers' or grandmothers' generations (again this could be attributed to the idea that fashion is cyclical).

Rhinestones are also popular with the masses. Whether it's for a formal occasion or a day at the park, rhinestones are certain to glam up anyone's wardrobe! Our generation is the pushing 50 crowd; we had more access to the rhinestones (both clear and colored) and beads. In today's market, it is getting harder and harder to find the quality rhinestone pieces that we like and appreciate. This does not necessarily mean that the rhinestones are not as popular; it is just that they are not as readily available as they once were. The quality pieces also command higher prices. People are still wearing them with great admiration.

Though the prices of rhinestones may be on the rise, one thing is for sure: jewelry (to paraphrase) is still a girl's best friend.

Ageless Accessories

(Right) Cigarette case that measures 2¼" by 3½". The sides and back are brushed in gold tone. The front is Lucite with gold lines forming a funky fresh retro starburst. Small rhinestones are sprinkled on every other line with the center of the star holding a larger stone. 1950s. Weighty. Unmarked. $70.00 – 100.00. (Left) Going gaga for gorgeous scents! Perfumer glass bottom is marked "MADE IN FRANCE." The glass is encased in metal. The top center holds a small turquoise cabochon. It came with the original funnel. $40.00 – 70.00.

(Left) Anybody know what time it is? This compact is stamped "OTTIS GRUN." The clock still works. Measures 2¾". Weighted. 1940s. $100.00 – 140.00. (Right) Put your lighters up! Ronson lighter, Woodbridge NJ. Vara Flame Lady Lite, International Pat. 1950s. Measures 2½". Black lighter with the cream colored flick stand and three flowers done in gold tone. Silver ribbons between the flowers. $35.00 – 55.00.

Commanding compact that will get anyone's attention. The original tag inside is signed "Riviera Creations." This compact was never used. Holds the original puff. The cover is 2½" by 2¾". 1940s. The rhinestones are handset in prongs. The center of each rectangle is made of ten rhinestone cabochons. Heavy! $150.00 – 210.00.

Glitzy, glitzy, snow-izty! Covered in rhinestones of all shapes, this snazzy compact is sure to make anyone look great in the mirror and among their friends! The stones are nice sizes and all hand set in prongs. 1940s to the early 1950s. The square is 3¼". It is hard for me to imagine that this piece is unsigned. $250.00 – 350.00.

3" square compact signed "VOLUPTÉ USA." Different shapes of stones are all glued into shallow cups. Weighted. 1940s to the early 1950s. Two baguettes are missing on the top right. $200.00 – 300.00.

(Left) Bedazzled belt measures 35". The crystals on the belt are bezel set, and the lining is pink. This belt would fit a smaller woman. 1970s. $40.00 – 60.00. (Right) The pencil measures 4" and is rose gold in tone. The silver roses are separated by a ring of rhinestones. 1930s. $50.00 – 90.00.

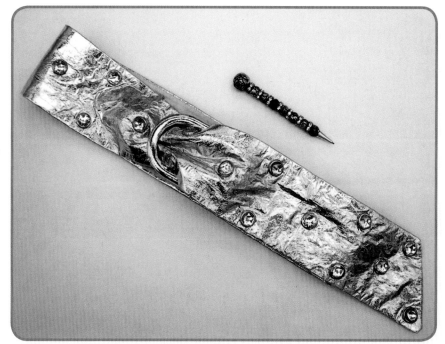

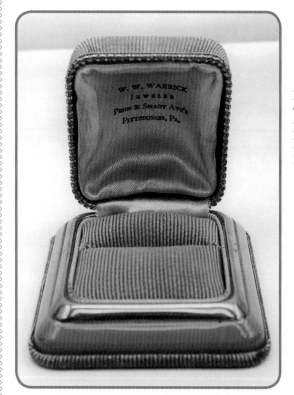

Rocking ring box. Inscribed
"W.W WARRICK JEWELER,
Penn & Shady Ave's,
Pittsburgh, PA." From the
1940s. $15.00 – 20.00.

The original paper tag on the mirror reads "Made
in Italy." The original powder puff is still in place.
A flattering picture on the front of this heavy
compact. 1940s. $80.00 – 120.00.

Beautiful, bold sunglasses. These black, round frames have rhinestones in the
center division and near the hinges. From the late 1950s. $20.00 – 40.00.

Mother-of-pearl square compact. Gold leaves in sand are mixed with pink, blue, and off-white seashells to make a robust flower. The flower is complemented by a blue bow; butterflies add beauty to this piece. Late 1940s to the early 1950s. $75.00 – 105.00.

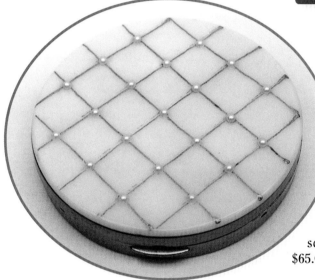

This outrageously beautiful compact has a white graph-like plastic top with faux pearls strategically placed at the squares' axes. 1950s. Unsigned. $65.00 – 95.00.

Made by Volupte U.S.A. This square compact is done in gold tone and has a design of a safari scene in a variety of colors. Hints of India. 1940s. $75.00 – 115.00.

Brilliant butterflies. Gold-tone base encompasses the butterfly painting signed by artist Holmes Grey; with its original box, signed "Stratton, England." Late 1940s to the mid-1950s. $85.00 – 125.00.

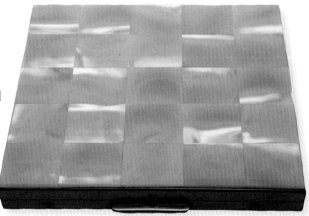

A smoking hot cigarette case! Mother-of-pearl plating. Twenty-five squares make up this pastel pretty. Unsigned. Mid-1940s to the late 1950s. $80.00 – 120.00.

Silver-tone cigarette case with a rhinestone top. Rhinestones are glued in shallow cups. Unsigned. 1940s to the 1950s. $80.00 – 125.00.

Daring dress clips have two rows of rhinestones set in nice oval shapes. 2¼". 1940s. Unsigned. $120.00 – 150.00.

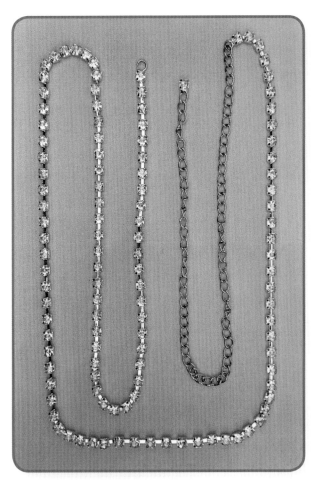

Bombshell belt measures 28¼". From the late 1950s. Fun and flashy! The adjustable chain measures 10¼". Unsigned. $100.00 – 140.00.

(Surrounding) White, plastic flower hair pins with gold-tone sternums that hold a single rhinestone. These are typically used in buns. Unsigned. 1950s. $40.00 – 80.00. (Center) White, plastic feathers with three flowers surrounding. In the centers of the flowers are single rhinestones. Unsigned. 1950s. $10.00 – 30.00.

(Left) The original powder is still in the box. A mirror is on the reverse side of this. 2". Unsigned. 1940s era. $65.00 – 115.00. (Center) A very feminine compact has a silver ball tip which controls the amount of powder sprinklings. Six holes are on the opposite side of the compact. Late 1940s. Signed "Richard Hudnut Paris." $70.00 – 120.00. (Right) This creative compact has a nicely engraved silver-tone top. A square is there for initials, but no initials are engraved in the square. Holds the original powder. 2¼". 1940s. Unsigned. $65.00 – 115.00.

Stud-ly steel cut shoe clips with a grosgrain backing. Art Nouveau. Measures 2¾" long by 2¼" wide. Unsigned. $110.00 – 150.00.

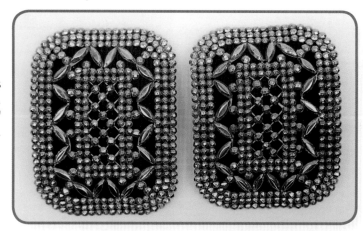

Come on baby light my fire! Sporty silver-tone lighter with a tennis player hitting a ball on the green enameled casing. Top and bottom right is signed "Manor." Left bottom reads "By WINDSOR Automatic Higher grade manor lite JAPAN." $45.00 – 85.00.

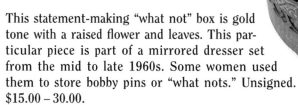

This statement-making "what not" box is gold tone with a raised flower and leaves. This particular piece is part of a mirrored dresser set from the mid to late 1960s. Some women used them to store bobby pins or "what nots." Unsigned. $15.00 – 30.00.

A gold rush compact with a floral design done in two tones of golden hues. Oval shaped. Inside mirror missing. 1960s. $50.00 – 70.00.

This 3¼" long by 2¾" wide compact is bedazzling to its beholder. The original powder puff is still inside. Gold "Revlon" name is stamped on a white background. When the compact opens, it reveals a full mirror. Late 1960s to the early 1970s. $95.00 – 115.00.

The powder puff inside this compact is white with a gold stamp reading "Max Factor." 2¾" by 2¾". Elgin American Made in the USA. Small and heavy. From the late 1950s. $95.00 – 115.00.

Glistening gold compact with a screen to filter the loose powder. The Lucite top is speckled in various tones of orange and yellow. Measures 2¾" by 2½". Mid-1950s to the late 1950s. $85.00 – 105.00.

A checkerboard of solid and hatched gold squares. Has a full mirror when opened. The original mint green powder puff is stamped "Elgin American." Measures 2¾" by 2¾". Signed "Elgin American Made in the USA." Late 1950s to the mid-1960s. Very heavy. $95.00 – 115.00.

Signed "HARRIET HUBBARD AGER" on the inside bottom right. This compact is simply bedazzling. From the early 1950s to the mid-1960s. Back has a rectangle area for engraving initials. Compact has a full size mirror when opened and a white, oval powder puff. Stamped in gold on the puff, "Helena Rubinstein." 2¾" by 2¾". $35.00 – 55.00.

Simple gold compact with the original mirror inside. Has a square powder puff with warm pink tones on both sides. A screen is implemented to filter loose powder. 2¼" long by 2⅛" wide. Unsigned. Early 1950s to the early 1960s. $55.00 – 85.00.

This dazzling compact has a gold brushed overlay on blue enameling. It looks Oriental. The bottom is done in gold with ribbing. Box had the compact in it when I acquired it. I don't think this is the original box. 2¾" by 2¾". Mid-1950s. Unsigned. $85.00 – 105.00.

Lightweight compact that has a full, round mirror when opened. A screen for loose powder is inside. When I purchased this, it was in the Fifth Avenue Zell Box. The back of the box reads "Proud Possession of the Particular Woman." Bottom of the compact is done in gold with ribbed circles. Unsigned. $70.00 – 90.00.

Bubble-licious beauty! This smoking cigarette case has 18 raised bubbles and 28 small red raised dots surrounding. 5¾" long by 2¾" wide. Signed "Ajestic USA" on the inside cigarette clip. 1950s. $115.00 – 125.00.

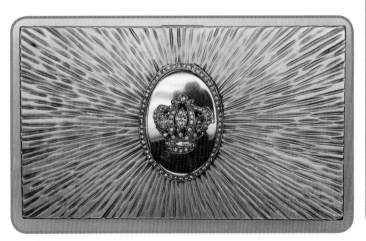

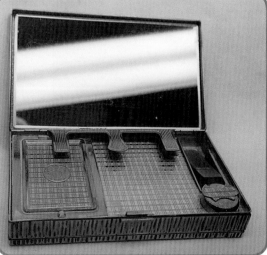

This cigarette case opens to a tri-fold. The gold holder, clip, and lighter are signed "Evans." A place for calling cards, powder, and lipstick are included all on one side. Complete with a full mirror. Elegant. $120.00 – 150.00.

A calmly curved cigarette case in gold wash over metal. Measures 5¾" by 3¾". Signed "Volupte USA" on each side of the cigarette holder. 1950s. $90.00 – 110.00.

Silver-tone cigarette case with a design that is reminiscent of the Orient. Nice detailing. When opened, there is an elastic holder on each side. 6¼" by 3¼". Unsigned, I'm shocked. 1950s. $100.00 – 140.00.

Highly flammable lighter makes my heart combust! Signed "Ronson" beneath the igniter and inside on the cigarette case's clip holder. 1950s. $75.00 – 105.00.

(Left) This lighter is completed in gold tone with white leather and nine small rhinestones that are prong set with one center. Signed "MASCOT" on the top left and bottom left. The bottom right is signed "Super Automatic Light Japan." $45.00 – 85.00. (Right) Four mother-of-pearl chunks overlay the gold top with a variety of colors and shapes of rhinestones. All are prong set by hand. Late 1940s. Unsigned. $50.00 – 90.00.

Look out Dynasty fans! This belt is 25½" long and 3½" wide. Done in silver, copper, and gold on a silver metallic. Each color has its own 2½" rows of chaton rhinestones. The center stone is 1¾" on the right of the belt. Two rhinestone chains suspend from the bottom of the belt. Late 1970s to the mid-1980s. $80.00 – 120.00.

This uptown chain belt made of gold links measures 51" long. A 13" double chain with five gold rings is suspended holding a flexible faux center pearl. 1970s. $40.00 – 70.00.

Pointedly pretty. Dazzling 1¾" show clips from the early 1930s. Unsigned. $35.00 – 65.00.

Stunning plastic hair clip is a bouquet of flowers. Each flower has a glued-in aurora borealis center. 1950s. $20.00 – 40.00.

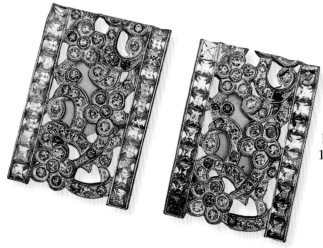

These dress clips are in silver tone and unfortunately, in poor condition. The baguettes and rhinestones are glued in. 1¾". Early 1930s. $25.00 – 55.00.

Gorgeous dress clips with pavé stones and small, ruby chaton-cut and baguette-cut stones. 2¼". Early 1930s era. $35.00 – 75.00.

Awesome Aurora Borealis

(Left) Aurora borealis crystals strung on wire make these stunning earrings. One crystal for the center does not have separators. ¾". Unsigned. 1940s to 1950s. $35.00 – 55.00. (Center) Four beads separate the four aurora borealis crystals. One crystal is used for the center. Yellow shades cast nicely. Measures ¾". Unsigned. $35.00 – 65.00. (Right) Signed "LAGUNA." Four beads separate the four aurora borealis crystals. The earrings are strung on wire with one crystal center. Back is filigree in silver tone. Absolutely smashing. ¾". 1940s to the 1950s. $40.00 – 70.00.

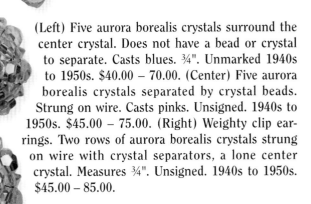

(Left) Five aurora borealis crystals surround the center crystal. Does not have a bead or crystal to separate. Casts blues. ¾". Unmarked 1940s to 1950s. $40.00 – 70.00. (Center) Five aurora borealis crystals separated by crystal beads. Strung on wire. Casts pinks. Unsigned. 1940s to 1950s. $45.00 – 75.00. (Right) Weighty clip earrings. Two rows of aurora borealis crystals strung on wire with crystal separators, a lone center crystal. Measures ¾". Unsigned. 1940s to 1950s. $45.00 – 85.00.

Pin and clip earrings set. The clip earrings have five aurora borealis crystals, each separated by a small round plastic bead. Strung on wire. Signed "Lisner®." 1940s to 1950s. $45.00 – 80.00.

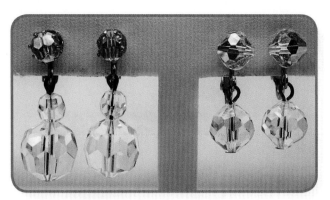

(Left) Two larger aurora borealis crystals dangle from a single, smaller aurora borealis crystal. 1½" long. 1940s to 1950s. $50.00 – 70.00. (Right) Clip earrings measure 1⅛". An aurora borealis crystal drops from the single crystal head. 1940s to 1950s. $35.00 – 65.00.

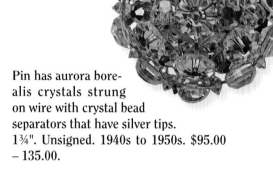

Pin has aurora borealis crystals strung on wire with crystal bead separators that have silver tips. 1¾". Unsigned. 1940s to 1950s. $95.00 – 135.00.

(Left) Clip earrings have three faux pearls with three aurora borealis crystals with one crystal in the center. Measures 1". Signed "TARA." 1940s to 1950s. $45.00 – 75.00. (Right) Seed pearls, gold beads, and aurora borealis compose these earrings. 1940s to the 1950s. $45.00 – 75.00.

(Left) Single strand of glass beads cut in diamond shapes. Metal rings are used to separate uniquely shaped beads. Signed "Sterling" on the clasp. Early 1930s. Measures 7¾". $135.00 – 175.00. (Center) Single strand of glass crystal beads. Faceting is great! Hand strung on wire. A silver bow for the clasp. Very heavy and sharp to touch. Unsigned. 1920s. 9" long. $160.00 – 210.00. (Right) Necklace is a single strand of glass crystals separated by a series of 4-3-2 metal beads. Hand strung on string. Barrel clasp. 8½" long. Unmarked. Late 1920s to early 1930s. $140.00 – 180.00.

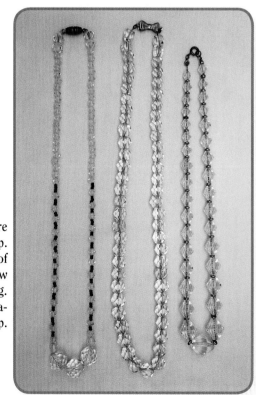

Necklace with two strands of sparkling aurora borealis crystals. Each crystal is separated by a gold metal ring that is strung tightly. Fishhook clasp with crystals suspended from a silver bar. Measures 5¾". Adjustable chain 3". Unmarked. Late 1940s to 1950s. $140.00 – 180.00. Clip earrings. Aurora borealis crystals strung on wire. Diamond-shaped beads form a star with a raised, center round crystal. One of a kind. ¾". Unmarked. 1940s to 1950s. $40.00 – 70.00.

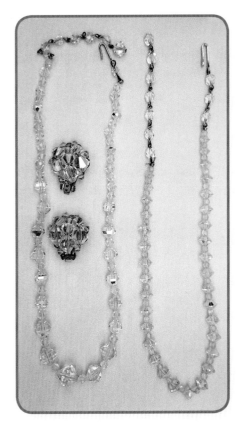

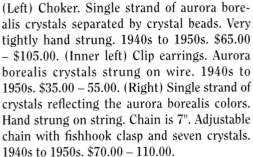

(Left) Choker. Single strand of aurora borealis crystals separated by crystal beads. Very tightly hand strung. 1940s to 1950s. $65.00 – $105.00. (Inner left) Clip earrings. Aurora borealis crystals strung on wire. 1940s to 1950s. $35.00 – 55.00. (Right) Single strand of crystals reflecting the aurora borealis colors. Hand strung on string. Chain is 7". Adjustable chain with fishhook clasp and seven crystals. 1940s to 1950s. $70.00 – 110.00.

(Left) Single strand of aurora borealis crystals separated by a crystal. Strung extremely tight. 5" long. 1½" adjustable chain. Unsigned. 1940s to 1950s. $85.00 – 120.00. (Right) Beautiful single strand of glass crystals. Each crystal is separated by a glass bead. Cut is greatly detailed, and there is a faint hint of aurora borealis. The fishhook clasp is signed "Laguna." Chain is hand strung on string. Measures 5¾". 1940s to the 1950s. Heavy. $90.00 –120.00.

For this necklace, each crystal is separated by a crystal bead. Two strands of stunning, graduated aurora borealis crystals drop from a silver-tone suspension with seven bright rhinestones glued in. Adjustable chain is 2⅛", and the necklace measures 7½". Signed "Lady Ellen" on the fishhook clasp. 1940s to the 1950s. $130.00 –180.00.

Three rows of brilliant aurora borealis crystals dangle from a silver-tone bar with four glued in rhinestones. One stone is missing on the left side of each silver-tone bar. The crystals are strung very tightly and each is separated by a crystal bead. Measures 6" in length and the fishhook clasp is 3½". Unsigned, yet uptown chic. 1940s to the 1950s. $150.00 – 200.00.

Three quite lovely strands of aurora borealis crystals are hooked onto a silver bar with an engraved design to finish the bar. Magnificent to wear in the sunshine! Silver-tone, adjustable, fishhook clasp is 3¼" long, while the necklace measures 6¾". Unsigned. 1940s to the 1950s. $150.00 – 200.00.

Three breathtaking rows of aurora borealis drop from a silver scroll-like top. A rather flexible piece. The fishhook clasp measures 3¾" in length, while the necklace is 6¼" long. Unsigned. 1940s to the 1950s. $120.00 – 160.00.

Suspended from a silver-tone bar are two strands of aurora borealis crystals in a graduated size. The colors reflect yellows, oranges, and more. Simply elegant. Necklace measures 6¼", and the adjustable fishhook clasp is 3¼". Unmarked. 1940s to the 1950s. $120.00 – 150.00.

A silver-tone scroll suspends the splendid, well-cut aurora borealis beads of this necklace. The three strands are sure to reflect the light with absolute brilliance. 7" long. 1940s to the 1950s. Unmarked. $135.00 – 185.00.

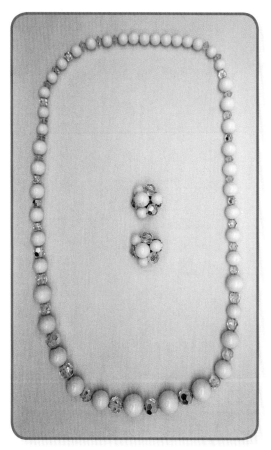

12½" necklace has white plastic beads which are separated by crystal, aurora borealis pieces. Matching clip earrings complete the set. The backing of the earrings is silver tone, with open filigree work. 1940s. Unsigned. $70.00 – 110.00.

(Left) Sparkling clip earrings. Eight crystals surround the large center aurora borealis. Measures ¾". Signed "GERMANY." 1940s. $40.00 – 70.00. (Center) Fine fish-wire strung crystals with a silver backing make up these unmarked, 1", 1940s clips. $40.00 – 70.00. (Right) Clip earrings with silver backings. Nice quality, aurora borealis crystals. The face crystals are tipped with silver pin. ¾". Unmarked. 1940s. $35.00 – 65.00.

(Left) Silver over metal on the back of these clip earrings. Each face crystal is tipped in silver pins. ¾". Unmarked. 1940s. $40.00 – 70.00. (Center) These, too, are silver over metal clip earrings. Well-worn backing on one earring is down to the metal. 1". Unmarked. 1940s. $40.00 – 70.00. (Right) Clip earrings, all round crystals are strung with black fine wire. 1". Unmarked. 1940s. $35.00 – 65.00.

(Left) Stunning screw-back earrings have a great cast of greens, and nine crystal beads surround the nicely faceted aurora borealis stone. ¾". Signed "STERLING." 1940s. $40.00 – 70.00. (Center) Clip earrings. Silver-tone backing. Dainty aurora borealis encompass a center aurora borealis stone. Unmarked. 1940s. $35.00 – 65.00. (Right) Clip earrings with silver backing. Eight fiery crystals surround the faceted center crystal. These were my Grandma Ault's, but she gave them to me. 1". Signed "GERMANY." 1940s. Priceless.

(Surrounding) Pair of gold-tone clip earrings. Faux pearl and aurora borealis clips with a drop of aurora borealis and pearls finished in gold. 1½". Unmarked. Late 1940s to the early 1950s. $45.00 – 75.00. (Center) Bracelet containing two strands of crystals with a gold button clasp. 3¼" closed. Unsigned. Early 1950s. $105.00 – 135.00.

(Outer) Necklace contains faux pearls and eight crystals on a string with a nicely faceted center crystal making nine. The lobster clasp is nicely detailed. 8". Unsigned. Early 1940s. $85.00 – 115.00. (Center) Silver clip earrings. Faux pearls with small aurora borealis in the center of the design. The pearls are tipped with a silver cap. ¾". Unmarked. 1940s. $30.00 – 65.00.

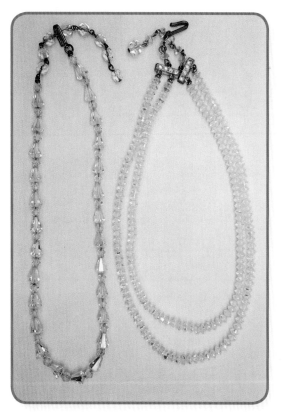

(Left) Necklace with a brass fishhook clasp. A single strand of tapered baguette crystals with the aurora borealis casting yellow and purple shades. 7" with 3½" of closure. Unmarked. 1940s. $110.00 – 140.00. (Right) Brass fishhook clasp attached to aurora borealis rhinestones on each side. Two strands of small crystals with all aurora borealis reminds me of a fresh snowfall. Unmarked. 1940s. $105.00 – 135.00.

(Left) A unique and elegant necklace. A large gold-tone fishhook clasp is attached to a 3" adjustable chain. White glass beads are strung on fine string. 6¼". Unmarked. 1940s. $115.00 – 145.00. (Right) Clip earrings. Silver-tone backing with fancy filigree work. Yellow-green pearls with wonderful, crystal aurora borealis centers. ¾". Unsigned. 1940s. $40.00 – 70.00.

A local lovely! Pennsylvania clip earrings, three strand necklace, and spiral bracelet. The earrings contain silver-tone backing. These pieces show excellent quality aurora borealis crystal beads. This set is in the original PT, Penn Traffic Co. Distinctive Johnstown, PA, box. This necklace shows great workmanship throughout this 6½" heavy beauty. 1¾" adjustable fishhook clasp, which is brass and signed "LAGUNA." The other side is a 3" adjustable chain. Five rhinestones begin to suspend 35 aurora borealis crystals. Earrings ¾" and signed "Laguna." Late 1940s. From Penn Traffic Co. Johnstown, PA. $225.00 – 325.00.

(Outer) Unique necklace. 2¼" adjustable gold-tone chain features lemon yellow glass beads. Measures 9¼". The clasp is signed "PAT PEND." Late 1950s to mid-1960s. $120.00 – 160.00. (Center) Pierced earrings. Three yellow crystal drops. Simple, and are dated back to the 1960s. $30.00 – 50.00.

(Left) Nicely faceted glass crystal beads. 1930s to the early 1940s. Hand strung on fish net. $150.00 – 200.00. (Right) A single strand necklace of graduated glass crystal aurora borealis beads with small crystals separating excellent faceted crystals. The center drop is drop-dead gorgeous! Measures 10½" with a 2¾" adjustable chain and fishhook clasp. Unsigned. 1940s. $120.00 – 150.00.

(Left) Clip earrings. Radiant colors of small aurora borealis stone suspended from a single hook. 1". Unsigned. Mid- to late 1950s. $35.00 – 45.00. (Right) Clip earrings. Small aurora borealis stone with three chain link drops holding the nice large faceted crystal. 1½". Unmarked. Mid- to late 1950s. $45.00 – 55.00.

(Left) Screw-on earrings. Top has a single, tiny rhinestone glued in. 1½" with three clear crystal beads graduated in size. Signed "JAPAN." Late 1940s to mid-1950s. $25.00 – 40.00. (Right) Clip earrings. Gold-tone backing. Three multicolored crystals with a single lightly colored crystal, held from a small crystal. 1½" long. Early 1950s. Unsigned. $45.00 – 75.00.

Outrageously gorgeous ocean blue crystals are suspended from gold bars. The bars have three rhinestones on each side. One rhinestone is missing. Measures 7". The chain and fishhook clasp is 3¼". $100.00 – 150.00.

(Left) Beads of four sizes converge to make this splendid, hand-strung necklace. A dark blue glass is used for the clasp. Wonderfully faceted. Mid-1920s to the early 1930s. 9⅛" long. $200.00 – 270.00. (Right) This nicely faceted necklace has three different sizes of graduated beads which are hand strung on string. Each bead is separated by a crystal. Mid-1920s to the early 1930s. Measures 7⅛". $190.00 – 250.00.

(Outer) This necklace has very lovely shaped crystals. Two rows of aurora borealis crystals droop from beautiful rhodium bars that have four pavé rhinestones in them. A heavy fishhook clasp with a 3" adjustable chain to close. Measures 6". 1940s. Unmarked. $120.00 – 160.00. (Inner) These clip earrings contain crystals which match the aforementioned necklace. They resemble a marquis style. ¾". Unmarked. 1940s. $45.00 – 85.00.

This necklace has two strands of crystals in rainbow colors. Gold beads separate the crystals. The clasp is a simply stunning, bold flower. 10¼" long. 1940s. Unsigned. $200.00 – 280.00.

(Outer) A fun conversation starter! Strands are suspended from gold bars with multicolored spacers. These pastel prism crystals are in an array of colors. Truly one of a kind. 1940s. Unsigned. 6¾". $170.00 – 230.00. (Inner) The clip earrings match the necklace. ¾". 1940s. Unmarked. $50.00 – 90.00.

(Outer) This necklace has a rhodium back with four pavé rhinestones, two strands of stunning aurora borealis crystals, and a ¾" adjustable chain and fishhook clasp, which is signed "Laguna." Necklace measures 6". 1940s. $120.00 – 170.00. (Inner) Tiny, delicate, aurora borealis crystals are on silver-tone clip earrings. ½". Unsigned. 1940s. $30.00 – 50.00.

(Left) Nicely cut, hand-strung crystals. Each crystal is separated by two beads and one tiny crystal. Measures 8¼". 1920s to the 1930s. Unsigned. $110.00 – 150.00. (Right) A cute choker with finely faceted crystals. Great detailing. Sharp to the touch. Necklace is a single strand of crystals. 1¾" adjustable chain with a large fishhook clasp. 1930s. Measures 6". $90.00 – 150.00.

(Left) 1940s beauty. A single strand of aurora borealis crystals with hints of yellow dominating the necklace. A large aurora borealis stone is set in the clasp. Measures 8¼". Unmarked. $120.00 – 160.00. (Right) A tightly strung choker with a single strand of aurora borealis stones. A large center stone is eye catching. 3" adjustable chain, brass fishhook clasp. Measures 6" long. Unsigned. 1940s. $95.00 – 135.00.

Three strands of aurora borealis crystals are strung on wire. Strands are suspended from a silver bar with five pavé rhinestones. One rhinestone is missing. 3½" adjustable chain, fishhook clasp. 1940s. Unsigned. $180.00 – 240.00.

Clasp is a prong-set marquis with a single, round rhinestone and two aurora borealis stones. Strung on fishing string. Purples, reds, grays, blues, and greens show through. Each bead has a black spacer. Measures 9½". Unsigned. 1940s. $90.00 – 150.00.

(Left) Beautiful bracelet! This sophisticated bracelet has two strands of aurora borealis crystals. A safety chain is on the clasp. Clasp connects the two small rings of pavé rhinestones. On the right side, two rhinestones are missing. 3½" long. Unsigned. $65.00 – 95.00. (Right) This Rengi necklace is fit for a princess. The reflections of color are brilliant in each crystal. Two strands of aurora borealis drop from a rhodium bar on each side. The bars have four pavé rhinestones each. Measures 6" long with a 2¾" adjustable chain clasp. 1940s. $140.00 – 180.00.

(Left) This uptown chic bracelet has crystals in graduated sizes, separated by crystals. 4¼". Signed "1-2012KCF." 1940s. $90.00 – 140.00. (Right) Choker made with aurora borealis crystals in multiple colors. Sizes are graduated. Strung on wire. Fishhook clasp is signed "Laguna." Measures 6" with a 3" adjustable chain. 1940s. $110.00 – 140.00.

(Left) Vibrant expansion bracelet with a double strand of aurora borealis crystals. Tightly strung. 1¾". 1940s. $80.00 – 130.00. (Center) These charming clip earrings have one large aurora borealis crystal dropping from a smaller one. Silver clips. Unsigned. Measures ¾". 1940s. $35.00 – 45.00. (Right) This tasteful bracelet is simply elegant. A single strand of aurora borealis crystals strung on wire. Simple crystal drop on each end. 2½" long. Unsigned. 1940s. $45.00 – 65.00.

(Left) These flexible clear beads twist and shake. Signed "Japan." 1940s. 1¼". $40.00 – 60.00. (Right) These clip earrings have aurora borealis crystals which drop like a waterfall. Many crystals are linked by a small chain. Clip is silver tone. 1½". Signed "Laguna." 1940s. $75.00 – 115.00.

The original Laguna box sits behind these pieces. (Left) Heavy, aurora borealis pin with crystals showing aquas, yellows, and pinks. Silver backing. 1940s. 2". Unsigned. $95.00 – 135.00. (Center) This circle pin is so sweet with its nicely sized beads. 1½" in diameter. 1940s. Unsigned. $90.00 – 130.00. (Right) This pin has aurora borealis crystals showing a lot of blues and aquas. Clear beads over silver tips. 1¼" in diameter. ¾" in depth. 1940s. Unsigned. $80.00 – 110.00.

(Left) Silver-tipped, aurora borealis crystals that are heavy and on a silver-tone backing. 1940s. Unsigned. 1½". $85.00 – 115.00. (Right) These clip earrings are hand strung on wire with gold tipping. 1⅛". 1940s. $75.00 – 105.00.

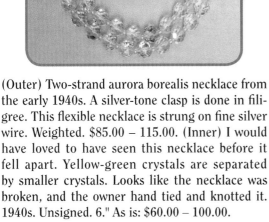

(Outer) Two-strand aurora borealis necklace from the early 1940s. A silver-tone clasp is done in filigree. This flexible necklace is strung on fine silver wire. Weighted. $85.00 – 115.00. (Inner) I would have loved to have seen this necklace before it fell apart. Yellow-green crystals are separated by smaller crystals. Looks like the necklace was broken, and the owner hand tied and knotted it. 1940s. Unsigned. 6." As is: $60.00 – 100.00.

All About Avon

This stunning set is sure to be the belle of the ball! Kenneth J. Lane necklace and matching clip earrings. Necklace measures 10½", earrings measure 1½". The back of each piece is stamped "K.J.L. for AVON" in a raised, round, gold-tone circle. The pearls are strung on a heavier white string. The drop of the necklace is weighty. The black glass is bezel set. Small, glued-in rhinestones border the glass. All with a gold burst around the stunning center. The earrings match the center. Late 1970s to the early 1980s. $100.00 – 130.00.

I cannot "leaf" you alone. Stamped "Louis Féraud PARIS" in a rectangular gold-tone bar on the back of the bottom right leaf. This came with matching leaf earrings. Late 1970s to the early 1980s. $75.00 – 105.00.

Think pink! Each piece is stamped "K.J.L. for AVON." The earrings measure 1", and the necklace measures 9¼". Two strands of faux pearls connect to the pretty pink flower. Set around the flower is the silver-tone border of pavé rhinestones. When I wear this set, I showcase the flower in the front of my neckline versus wearing the flower as the clip. It is simply too pretty to hide! Late 1970s to early 1980s. $95.00 – 125.00.

Stamped on the bottom of each gold-tone seashell is "K.J.L. for AVON." Holy Cape Coral! The coral twist is done in two-tone colors of coral with small gold-tone beads in four strands. Measures 8¼". The seashell is 2". Matching earrings came with this set. Quite weighty. The original box has instructions showing six different ways to wear the necklace. How versatile! 1980s. $100.00 – 130.00.

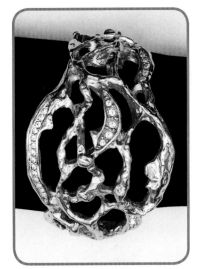

This gold-tone vine style bracelet is stamped "ELIZABETH TAYLOR E AVON" in a raised gold-tone oval on the back. It is hinged to open. Weighty. 1980s. $95.00 – 135.00.

Each and every piece is weighty. Excellent craftsmanship. The necklace measures 11¼". The chains are gold electroplate. They are done in links and measure 4¾". The necklace's cabochons are done in three shapes with green, blue, cranberry, and purple colors. Each is bordered by a heavy gold-tone rope design. The cranberry oval shape is stamped "K.J.L. for AVON." Each earring measures 1¼" and is signed on the clip "AVON." The bracelet measures 8¾" and is signed "AVON." Great set to wear with jeans! Late 1970s to the 1980s. $130.00 – 160.00.

A timeless favorite of mine. "BARRERA for AVON" is signed on each piece of this parure. I have worn this so much it is a wonder it doesn't have a worn, aged look. The heart-shaped earrings measure 1¾". Brushed gold open filigree work with small rhinestones glued in deep cups. The necklace is done in three sections. The sides are in a 1½" scrolling design and hinged to the center drop heart. Each side has the link chains and a fishhook clasp to close. Late 1970s early 1980s. $90.00 – 120.00.

(Left) Superb colors are used for this arrangement. A pendant that converts to a necklace. Signed "NR AVON." The gold-tone link chain measures 14½", pendant measures 2½". Four topaz emerald shaped cabochons with four faux pearls set in gold caps with a center of a bezel set amethyst. Late 1970s to the 1980s. $55.00 – 95.00. (Right) Bracelet in gold tone that borders five different colors of cabochons. Early 1990s. $35.00 – 55.00.

Two stands of faux pearls measure 7½" with a gold link chain measuring 3½" and a fishhook clasp to close. The drop is 4" long by 2½" wide. The earrings match the drop. Looks like royalty to me; this set is fit for Duchess Fergie. Each piece is signed "AVON." 1980s. $115.00 – 145.00.

Matching earrings and brooch. "©
BARRERA for AVON" is signed on each
clip earring. 2½" long. The top looks
like antiqued gold with the tip done in
a marquee. Seven small round rhinestones are glued in shallow cups. Five
seed pearls are glued to the cup. The
center is a bezel set red cabochon. The
blue ball drop is capped in gold. 1980s.
Weighted. This brooch converts to a
necklace. The original chain is unlo-
catable. It measures 3½". Signed "©
BARRERA for AVON." For the set:
$100.00 – 140.00.

Hearts afire! Each piece is signed "©
AVON." 1980s. Gold electroplate with
pavé rhinestones set in the heart pin
and matching clip earrings. The earrings measure 1¼" with the pin measuring 2½". This might have been
a Valentine's day seller for the company. This is pleasing for the February
fashion season. $55.00 – 85.00.

(Left) Necklace. 1970s. $70.00 – 100.00.
(Right) Wide gold electroplate bracelet
from the 1970s. The center is a 1½" off-
white square. On the back of this it is
stamped "© AVON." $50.00 – 80.00.

Cute collar! This necklace is stamped "GALLERY ORIGINAL" on the back of the gold electroplate collar. The center has horizontal and vertical scrolls. 1980s. $55.00 – 85.00.

A flexible work. The clasp of the two strand, 19", gray necklace is stamped "© BARRERA for AVON." The clasp converts to a brooch and has a gray drop. The 1½" gold-tone clip earrings are both signed at the clasp. Late 1980s to the early 1990s. $70.00 – 100.00.

Signed "Louis Féraud Paris" on the back of the center of this 9" necklace. The silver cabochon is closed on the back and finished in gold tone. Small cabochon clip earrings are bordered in gold tone. They are unmarked. 1984. $60.00 – 90.00.

Looks like Louis Féraud but is unsigned. Four strands of hand-strung dark seed beads are on a thread that matches the beads. They are done in four sections connected by two sets of gold-tone rings on each side. The clasp is finished to match the sides. Measures 18⅛". $55.00 – 85.00.

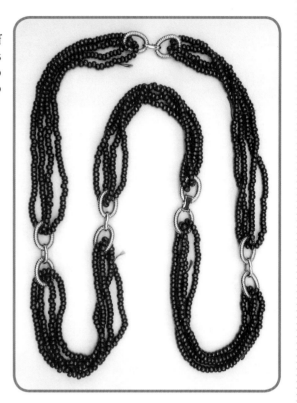

Louis Féraud pearl and onyx necklace measures 8¼". Hand strung on white thread. Small black beads separate the pearls. Six small gold-tone beads cap the onyx. Gold barrel clasp is used to close. 1984. $45.00 – 75.00.

Go Steelers! Show your Pittsburgh pride in this black and gold beauty. The original tag is on this beauty. 19½" of black and gold. The drop is 1¾". A gold-tone barrel clasp is used to close. This would be pretty around the holidays or to wear to any Pittsburgh event! 1984. Matching clip earrings are 2". Signed $55.00 – 85.00.

Each item is marked "© BARRERA for AVON." Clip earrings measure 1¾". Black cabochons are bezel set in each earring with four small rhinestones set in shallow cups. The necklace can be hinged together in the bottom center. Three black cabochons are bezel set with 10 small rhinestones sprinkled about. Late 1980s to the early 1990s. $75.00 – 105.00.

This beautiful blue necklace converts to a pin. The pearl center highlights the blue enameling with the faux turquoise and rhinestones set in the gold-tone cups. Measures 3¼", the chain measures 14½". The back is signed and hard to read. Each matching clip earring is signed and measures 2¼". Nice weighted set. Late 1980s to the early 1990s. $85.00 – 125.00.

(Top) Clip earrings measure 3⅛". Hurts my eyes to look at all of the gold! Stunning is not even close to what these are! Rhinestones are glued in shallow cups and scattered throughout the earrings. Gold electroplate. Heavy. $55.00 – 95.00. (Bottom) 1¾" clip gold-tone earrings. Nice door knockers. $45.00 – 65.00. Each piece is signed "© BARRERA for AVON," and each is from the late 1980s to the early 1990s.

(Top) Each earring is signed "© BARRERA for AVON." They are in the original box called Holiday Splendour. They are heavy! Each measures 3½". The gold-tone flower has nine rhinestones glued into shallow cups. This connects to a snowball then drops to the glass. Late 1980s to the early 1990s. $65.00 – 85.00. (Bottom) 4½" clip earrings. The top is open filigree with three flowers, and each have one small rhinestone set in the center to frame the center flower. Each has a center rhinestone that drops to the lone flower. Each earring's drop is signed "© BARRERA for AVON." Nice filigree work. Late 1980s to early 1990s. $65.00 – 85.00.

This piece is reminiscent of Easter time. Parure of clip earrings and necklace. This set would be pretty for the spring season. Each item is signed "© BARRERA for AVON." Three weighted chain links close in the back of the necklace. The center measures 2¼". Light purple cabochons and small pink rhinestones complement the gold electroplate. The chain closed measures 9". Earrings are 2". Nice craftsmanship on this set. $120.00 – 150.00.

Pretty for summer. The necklace is done in three sections of filigree design. Each section has stars. The adjustable chain has a fishhook clasp to close. Parure of clip earrings and necklace. Late 1980s to the early 1990s. Each piece is signed "© BARRERA for AVON." The earrings measure 1½". $105.00 – 135.00.

Parure of clip earrings and pin. Earrings measure 3¼" and can be worn as a single flower or flower on top with the oval loop. Flower pin measures 4¼". Quite colorful enameling. This is definitely summertime fun. Late 1980s to the early 1990s. Each item is signed "© BARRERA for AVON." $80.00 – 120.00.

In 1984, two stars were born when Louis Féraud introduced FANTASQUE perfume, and I introduced on November 17, Katie, my daughter! This is Louis Féraud's perfumer necklace in the original cloth bag. The rope measures 17". The base is 1½" by 1¾". $55.00 – 85.00. The left features the original parfume that made its debut with the perfume.

All three pieces are signed "K.J.L. for AVON." Two strand, faux, large pearl necklace with a gold-tone lion clasp. Hand strung on heavy white thread. Measures 9". Earrings measure 1¾". Earrings came pierced or clip. 1990s. $100.00 – 150.00.

The faux pearl necklace measures 11¾". The clasp is finished in a marquee done in filigree. The black enameled bow with a gold frame is sophisticated looking. Earrings came in either pierced or clip. They measure 1¼". Each is signed "K.J.L. for AVON." 1990s. $90.00 – 130.00.

Parure. Eight strands of black beads hand strung on fish wire. Measures 8". Panther clasp is signed "K.J.L." Clip earrings signed "K.J.L." Brooch is signed "K.J.L. for AVON." Measures 2¼". Each panther is comprised of pavé rhinestones with emerald eyes and black glass spots. The brooch has a sapphire collar. The clasp and earrings have pavé rhinestones in a ring. The purse is 6½" by 4¼". The nylon rope handle measures 24½" and fits into the purse. The fabric that lines the bag is signed "Kenneth Jay Lane" in gray throughout the purse. The fabric is black. The clasp matches the earrings. Boldly beautiful. 1990s. $350.00 – 450.00.

This Kenneth Jay Lane purse is lined in black fabric. It is signed "Kenneth Jay Lane" in gray throughout the purse. The handle measures 6". The three square pavé rhinestones attach to the clips for the handle. The handle can be tucked back into the bag so you may carry it as a clutch. Either way it is quite appealing. The clasp matches. Paure consists of a collar and earrings. The earrings are pavé rhinestone hoops. The collar necklace measures 7½". This was for Christmas 2004. Each earring is marked "AVON SP." The collar is marked "K.J.L." on one clasp, and the other is signed "SP AVON." $225.00 – 325.00.

(Left) Not my favorite piece because I don't like snakes. The snake measures 3". Red cabochons are used for eyes, with blue cabochons on the body, and pavé rhinestones set in gold tone. Signed on the back "KJL for AVON." 1980s. $75.00 – 105.00. (Bottom right) KJL Bumble bee pin. Pavé rhinestones on the wings, yellow stones on the spine, emeralds for the eyes. $60.00 – 90.00. (Top right) Panther brooch stamped "KENNETH © LANE." Measures 2¼". Pavé rhinestones with black enameling and an emerald eye. $70.00 – 100.00.

(Top) 1" weighted pierced earrings done in black enameling with pavé rhinestones set in gold tone. The center is an oval emerald. 1990s. $70.00 – 100.00. (Center) Signed "GIORGIO." This lion hinged cuff bracelet is done in black enameling and pavé rhinestones set in gold tone. 1990s. $125.00 – 155.00.

If I were to guess, I would say this was an award or gift for the district managers. The choker is 12" with an adjustable chain with a fishhook clasp to close. Five strands of small pearls are hand strung on string. The center is done in silver tone with pavé rhinestones. The back center is stamped "KJL." The center, which could be a brooch, measures 3¼", and is stamped "KJL." Each earring is signed "KJL." The watch is black ribbed fabric with the center done in pavé rhinestones in silver tone. On the back of this, it is signed "Kenneth Jay Lane." $375.00 – 475.00.

(Outer) Choker is signed "KJL AVON" on the back of the center. Just like a Rolex, gold and silver. Nice weight. $75.00 – 105.00. (Top center) Ring is signed "AVON." $45.00 – 65.00. (Center) Earrings are pierced, and each clasp is stamped "AVON." Light weight. All are from the late 1970s to the early 1980s. $40.00 – 50.00.

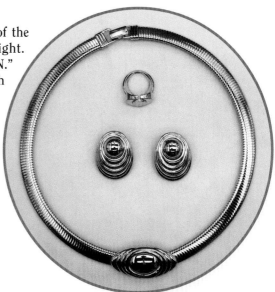

(Left) KJL for AVON elephant just in time for the 2008 elections! The elephant measures 2". Its body is done in gold and bone with seven small rhinestones glued in each side with two on the top. Gold link chain measures 14½". 1980s. $80.00 – 130.00. (Right) Gold-tone rose with pavé stones from the 1980s. $65.00 – 95.00.

Look out fireworks on the 4th of July! 2¾" of bursting fiery pavé rhinestones show off so well with the gold-tone sprigs set between each silver sprig. A 1" center, open backed, faux ruby is hand set in prongs. Signed "KJL." 1980s. $85.00 – 105.00.

Down by the seashore is where we go every 4th of July. All pieces are stamped "KJL." Faux turquoise, pearls, and cabochons are all glued in shallow cups. Brooch measures 3". The earrings are pierced. 1980s. $100.00 – 140.00.

Summertime fun! The 12½" necklace has all the beachy signs. The earrings measure 2" and are flexible. The necklace is signed "KJL for AVON" on the center star. Each back of the clip earrings is signed. Late 1980s to the mid 1990s. $100.00 – 140.00.

Double strand of black beads measure 9", with a white flower clasp. The center of the flower is gold tone with small rhinestones. The pierced earrings are done in black flowers. Each piece is signed "K.J.L. for AVON." The original box reads 1991. $120.00 – 160.00.

Parure. 15" of double strands of blue beads. Small gold beads separate in a series of five. To the clasp, they separate in a series of three. Gold-tone rams' heads with emerald eyes to close. Matching ram earrings. Each is signed "K.J.L. for AVON." $140.00 – 180.00.

(Outer) 9½" double strands of faux baroque pearls tightly strung on heavy string. The butterfly is enameled in peach and vanilla. Three small rhinestones are set in shallow cups. Gold-tone swirls frame the butterfly. Matching pierced earrings. Each is signed "K.J.L. for AVON." $125.00 – 155.00. (Inner) 3" dragonfly with bezel set pink glass. The spine is done in small rhinestones. Framed in gold tone. Signed "K.J.L. for AVON." $75.00 – 105.00.

Each piece is signed "K.J.L. for AVON." The original box reads "2000." A 17" single strand coral is hand strung on white string. The clasp for the necklace converts to a brooch. The center cabochon is light pink with the border of butter and peach enameling. Earrings to match. $95.00 – 135.00.

(Left) Silver bow with pavé rhinestones measures 3". Signed "KJL" on the back. 1980s. $70.00 – 100.00. (Right) This 3¼" pin is signed "KJL." Late 1980s to the early 1990s. $65.00 – 105.00.

(Top) Earrings KJL gold-tone pavé rhinestones. $40.00 – 60.00. (The set) Glam gold! Lustrous bow pin and clip earrings. Gold tone with rhinestones. Original selling price was $39.99 (for the set) when introduced, which was the late 1980s to the early 1990s. $85.00 – 125.00.

Necklace measures 9¼" and the matching clip earrings are 1". This set is unsigned, but the bold blue and weighty beads set on gold tone appear as though it should be signed. Gold spacers separate blue beads on the lower half of the necklace. The pearl drop is accentuated by pavé rhinestones and glorious gold shades. The earrings match the drop. Mid-1990s. $75.00 – 105.00.

Stunning silver! Lustrous bow pin and clip earrings. Silver tone with rhinestones. Original selling price was $39.99 (for the set) when introduced, which was the late 1980s to the early 1990s. $85.00 – 125.00.

(Top) Beautiful onyx-like earrings with a surrounding golden scroll design. ¾". $20.00 – 25.00. (Bottom) 1½" cameo clip-on earrings. Pearls are used as side accent pieces. $25.00 – 35.00.

Silver-tone compact that measures 2¾" from the Gallery Collection. Has three beautiful sapphire colored square stones in Art Deco like design with the original dust cloth. $50.00 – 70.00.

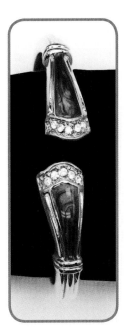

Lovely little bracelet that's signed "KJL." The springtime bracelet has wonderfully rich gray cabochons on top of the cuffs, which is offset by small, delicate pavé rhinestones. $45.00 – 65.00.

Signed "KJL for Avon." Pretty panther with green eyes and a pavé rhinestone t-zone. Matching pierced earrings. Lovely gray beads complement this 10" necklace. Super weighty. $95.00 – 135.00.

Baubles of Beads

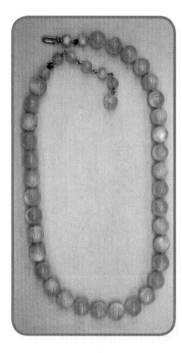

For imitation glass, this is certainly splendid. Signed "Japan." Necklace from the 1940s. Measures 9" when closed, the adjustable chain measures 3½". The off-white beads are hand knotted on white string. $75.00 – 115.00.

An amalgamation of materials. This 24" necklace has matching 1¾" screw on earrings. The pattern is aurora borealis with beads in two sets with a molded plastic beads tipped in gold tone that comprises the connectors, followed by a bead, and then an aurora borealis with a bead then a large carved glass stone with gold etching. Unmarked set. 1930s. $95.00 – 135.00.

No need to bare skin to get these French Quarter-like gems. Late 1920s, amethyst, and citrine glass necklace. It is hand strung on fish wire. Four barrel-shaped amethyst stones fall to the base of the necklace. These colors are unusual together and reminiscent of Mardi Gras. Measures 13". Unsigned. $105.00 – 145.00.

This piece features a lovely springtime canvas of colors. Measures 12".
White and pink glass beads have a smaller bead set on each side with
blues and yellows in a whimsical design. The base has a pink glass
bead with three small green dots on both sides of the bead. From the
1940s. $90.00 – 140.00.

Plain Jane, I think not! Puffy and
perfectly pretty are these 8½" of
opalescent hand-blown glass beads
that are separated with faux pearls.
1930s. Hand strung on fine silver
wire. $110.00 – 170.00.

Party in the beads! 1960s molded plastic necklace measures 14".
Five larger beads are filled with confetti and separated by six silver
saucer shapes. The two colors of yellow beads are set off with the
silver plastic beehive shape connected to a gold-tone saucer. Hand
strung on fine silver wire. Unmarked. $65.00 – 95.00.

(Left) Orange you glad that such magnificent necklaces still exist? 12" orange glass beads separated by a small crystal bead. Tightly strung. 1930s. Unmarked. $110.00 – 160.00. (Right) Just like the brilliant shades found in nature's own cranberry bogs. 1920s, unsigned cranberry and white necklace. Glass beads are two toned. Strung tightly. The ends are tied string. Measures 7½". $110.00 – 140.00.

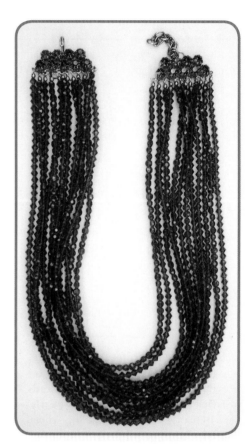

Prom perfect? Absolutely. Steal your date's eyes and heart when you don such eclectic apparel. Closed, this black beauty measures 8½" to the center fringe drop. Weighted. Unsigned. A fishhook clasp with 3½" of adjustable black glass beads to close. 1940s. A single strand of black glass beads with fringe of a bugle bead connecting to a small crystal bead then to a glass bead. Flexible. $180.00 – 220.00.

A multi-strand necklace of eye-catching, tranquil blues. This 1940s necklace measures 10". Signed at the base of the fishhook "MADE IN AUSTRIA." Three shades of blue with delicate Austrian crystals are hand strung on heavy silver wire. Weighted. Excellent craftsmanship. The clasp is finished with a row of five larger blue stones with four larger blue stones on top of the five. Both are hand set in silver-tone prongs. The chain measures 1¾" with a hook. $195.00 – 255.00.

Signed twice "MARVELLA" on the fish-hook clasp and stamped "MARVELLA" on the clasp's gold-tone base. Measure 8". The adjustable clasp measures 2". A gold-tone bow-like bar begins the five strands of green glass crystals that are hand strung. The crystals are in a series of two separated by a small gold colored flat bead. They are in two different sizes. 1940s. $150.00 – 200.00.

For a fairy tale wedding, invest in a set of these beads that are perfect for the bride to be and the bridesmaids alike. This five strand aurora borealis measures 8" with an adjustable chain measuring 3½". A silver-tone fishhook clasp is used to close. Weighted. The crystals are all hand strung. They are strung tightly. The colors reflect lemons, pinks, and purple reds. The five strands are attached to a silver-tone open bar. 1940s. $145.00 – 195.00.

Measures 6½" with the adjustable chain measuring 2½". A fishhook clasp is used to close these aurora borealis beads. The three strands are attached to a silver-tone bar that holds four, small, glued-in rhinestones. The beads are flat and separated by a small plastic bead. Tightly strung by hand. Late 1930s to early 1940s. Reflects the prettiest pastels. $95.00 – 135.00.

(Outer) Unsigned, and I am surprised! This 1960s, two strand, faux pearl necklace is hand knotted on a heavy string. Measures 17". Heavy weight! Each strand is off set with black faux pearls. Each is separated with a gold-tone spacer. The center drop is the black faux pearl. Matching pierced earrings (in the very center of the photo). The clasp is gold wash with a raised design. $100.00 – 140.00. (Inner) Single strand of orange beads. Hand strung on heavy string. The beads have two gold-tone beads on each side. The clasp is stamped on the back "HONG KONG." The front is finished with a faux tiger eye bordered with a gold-tone ring. Late 1940s to early 1950s. Measures 11½". $65.00 – 95.00.

(Top) Stamped "De ville" on each gold-tone bar. The adjustable chain measures 3¼". Fishhook clasp to close. Necklace measure 7". Three strands of beads are strung tightly on wire. The greens, blues, and golds enhance the fun of this necklace. I can picture this worn with a nice swimsuit on the beach. Late 1940s early 1950s. $70.00 – 100.00. (Bottom) Fishhook clasp is signed "JAPAN." The adjustable chain measures 3". Three strands of three shades of green plastic beads are hand strung on wire. The necklace measures 7". Pretty for St. Patrick's day. 1950s. $65.00 – 95.00.

Weighty glass beads in citrus tri-colors are strung tightly on string with an adjustable fishhook clasp to close. 1930s. $100.00 – 150.00.

Late 1960s to the early 1970s. Bountiful borealis! Clip earrings and necklace set made of faux pearls with citrine-colored molded plastic and plastic aurora borealis. The necklace measures 7", and the earrings are 1⅛". $35.00 – 55.00.

A hot mess! Each of the two sections have four rows of two small yellow beads with a small staple gold-tone chain with tiger's eyes tipped with gold-tone cups. The clasp is composed of seven faux cabochons in a brilliant tiger's eyes shade. The piece is crudely stamped "JAPAN." Measures 12". $65.00 – 105.00.

Looks like Hobé, but unmarked. This set is high quality with all beads hand strung on fish wire. The lemon colored glass beads are tipped in gold-tone cups. The glass beads are shaped like a tulip and are connected to yellow aurora borealis beads. A gold-tone flower clasp is used to close the necklace. 1950s. $100.00 – 150.00.

(Top) 1950s unsigned necklace. Two rows of greens and gold faux pearls with each pearl capped in yellow and white plastic. Hand strung. They are strung tightly. $55.00 – 75.00. (Bottom) This 8" oldie goldie is weighty! 1950s. Unsigned. Gold filigree beads, gold painted beads, and aurora borealis comprise this darling necklace that is also highlighted by a warm shade of chocolate, which has matching clip-on earrings. $75.00 – 105.00.

Unmarked. Three strands of three colors of green beads are completed with a gold-plated flower clasp that has a green bead center. A fishhook clasp is used to close. $40.00 – 60.00.

Two strands of tri-colored green beads measure 10". Early 1960s and is unsigned. Dazzling gold tone with transparent beads to complete the fishhook clasp. $30.00 – 50.00.

Weighted bracelet. Spiral with five rows of black beads strung on wire. Unmarked. 1960s. $45.00 – 85.00.

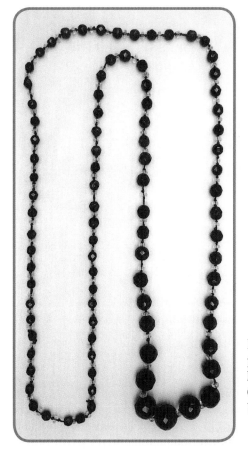

(Outer) Jet glass beads. Strung on a very fine linked wire with a large bead on the clasp. 12¼". Mid to late 1920s. $130.00 – 180.00. (Center) Jet glass beads. Hand strung on black string with a silver clasp with cross design. 7¾". Unsigned. Mid to late 1920s. $110.00 – 140.00.

Roaring 1920s. This fabulous 22" necklace was probably donned by the flappers of the 1920s. The black jet glass beads are hand strung and knotted. Clear spacers were inserted between each bead. Unsigned. $150.00 – 200.00.

Grand necklace and clip earrings set. Gold-tone scroll bar with two strands of plastic beads in light to dark shades of cranberry with dark aurora borealis. 7". 3½" adjustable chain. Earrings measure 1½". Each of the earrings and the fish-hook clasp are signed "West Germany." Early 1950s. For the set: $140.00 – 190.00.

A tasteful, 2001 Christmas gift from my husband. Light pink to deeper shades of grape with plastic beads in three strands. Three marvelous strands drop from a gold-tone bar; each bead has a gold cap. Adjustable chain measures 2¾", necklace is 8", and the earrings are 1¼". The earrings' and the necklace's fishhook clasps are signed "W. Germany." Early 1950s. No value assigned.

Sophisticated clip earrings and necklace couple. Three strands of yellow and coral plastic beads are suspended from a gold-tone, plastic bar. Each bead is separated by a faux seed pearl. Darling for summertime fun in the sun! Earrings measure 1". 3" adjustable chain. 8¾" necklace. The earrings and the fishhook clasp are signed "Japan." 1950s. $85.00 – 125.00.

Remarkable summer necklace and clip earrings duo. Three strands of magnificent coral beads that are separated by small, gold, roped beads. Fishhook clasp. 6¼" necklace with a 3" adjustable chain. Unsigned. 1950s. $110.00 – 160.00.

Hand-strung, citrine-colored and darker coral beads have gold beads to separate approximately every 3¼". Clasp is six beads with a molded plastic citrine for the center. Earring is 1⅛". Necklace is 12". Both the necklace clasp and earrings are signed "Made in Western Germany." Early 1950s. $140.00 – 200.00.

Three-tone purple, plastic beads are strung on heavy string. The strands are dropped from a silver-tone swirl design. 7" long, 1¼" adjustable chain, and the earrings are ¾". Earrings signed "Japan." Late 1950s. $80.00 – 120.00.

Go Steelers! Let's hear it for the black and gold! Bold beads! Cute clips! The beads are graduated in size, and each is separated by a golden swirl bead. Earrings, 2¼"; necklace, 8"; adjustable chain, 2¾". Early 1960s. Unsigned. $130.00 – 200.00.

(Outer) Beautiful necklace that is signed "Japan" on the fishhook clasp. Measures 8", the adjustable chain is 3¼". Late 1950s. $60.00 – 100.00. (Inner) Earrings signed "Miriam Haskell." 1960s. Baroque pearls, bezel-set in gold tone. $100.00 – 150.00.

Katie bought this necklace for me in Saltsburg, Pennsylvania. Great for a summer day in southern Florida. Detailing is typical of Hong Kong. A pattern of two or three beads are then separated by a flower. Clasp signed "Hong Kong." Great detail. Early 1950s. 9⅛". No value assigned.

Necklace signed "©Kramer." Single strand of plastic beads are hand strung on string. 8½" long, 3" adjustable chain. 1950s. $100.00 – 140.00.

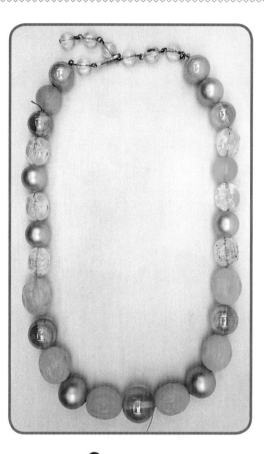

Necklace strung on rope. Denim blue wooden beads on a 7¼" strand. The tag reads "Cathy & Marsha for Catherine Stein." Original price of $23.00. 1970s. $50.00 – 90.00.

(Left) Necklace of pear and round-shaped white glass on a hand-knotted string separated by two discs. Necklace measures 6½" with a 3¼" chain and a fish-hook clasp. Signed "MJ WESTERN GERMANY." Late 1940s to early 1950s. $105.00 – 135.00. (Right) Hand-strung black glass beads on a black heavy thread. A lot of give between the beads. Looks like Germany though it is unmarked. 6" with a 2¼" adjustable chain. Late 1940s to the early 1950s. $105.00 – 145.00.

Necklace and clip earrings set from the 1970s to the early 1980s. Oh, so *Dallas* and *Dynasty*! Notice one strand is missing. Is this intentional from the previous owner? Strung on string, separated by gold plastic beads. Necklace is 7¾" with adjustable 4⅛" chain. Earrings are 2½" long. Unmarked. $55.00 – 85.00.

Eighteen strands of hand-strung beads measure 7½". The gold-tone floral clasp has a flower's center holding small aqua-colored stones. The leaves hug the strands of beads. Unsigned. 1980s. $160.00 – 200.00.

Magically minty! Silver-tone necklace. 1970s. Measures 8¾" and is unmarked. A fishhook clasp closes this silver-tone beauty of mint green beads. All are hand strung on a double rope. Hand knotted. $100.00 – 150.00.

Seeing red! Thirty strands of red seed beads. The original tag reads "Pomeroy's $20.00." 1970s. Measures 15". Silver-tone beads and a fishhook clasp. $140.00 – 200.00.

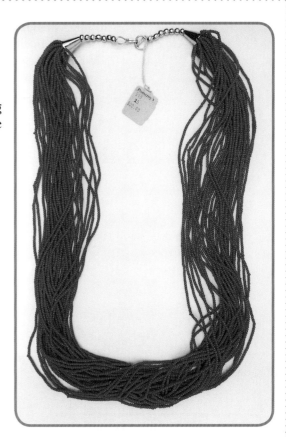

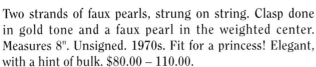

Two strands of faux pearls, strung on string. Clasp done in gold tone and a faux pearl in the weighted center. Measures 8". Unsigned. 1970s. Fit for a princess! Elegant, with a hint of bulk. $80.00 – 110.00.

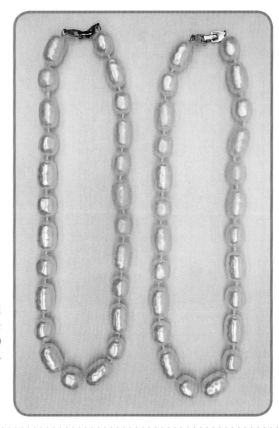

Double trouble! (Left) 8" faux pearl necklaces. Single strand of larger sized pearls strung on a rope. Clasp is gold tone with two chaton cut rhinestones. Unmarked. 1950s. $35.00 – 65.00. (Right) 9" long and a silver-tone clasp is the only difference from the left identification. $35.00 – 65.00.

This three-strand, marvelous, faux white pearl necklace is sure to bring the house down. 9" with a 1¾" clasp signed "JAPAN." Clasp is gold filigree with the back strung on fine wire. Late 1950s to the early 1960s. $85.00 – 135.00.

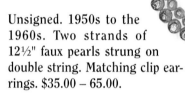

Unsigned. 1950s to the 1960s. Two strands of 12½" faux pearls strung on double string. Matching clip earrings. $35.00 – 65.00.

TRIFARI also signed a lowercase "t" on the right side of the adjustable chain, as was used in this particular piece. 8¼" with a 2¾" adjustable chain with a fishhook clasp. Heavy necklace. Two sizes of faux pearls separated by a small gold-tone ring. Gold-tone barrels embrace the pearls in a pattern of three. Mid-1950s to the early 1960s. $65.00 – 115.00.

Single strand of butterscotch plastic beads. Strung on a string of a matching color. Imitates glass. Measures 15½". Late 1940s to mid-1950s. Unsigned. $70.00 – 110.00.

Exquisite necklace and matching clip earrings. Four strands of three tones in greens, with golds and aurora borealis. Each bead is separated by a small gold bead. Multiple textures make up the beads. Excellent weight. Measures 8¾" with a 3" adjustable chain. Original paper is red and gold. Tag reads "LaBelle $4.00 plus tax." The clip earrings and fishhook clasp are signed "Japan." 1950s. $120.00 – 170.00.

Necklace and matching clip earrings. Three strands of multicolored plastic beads are strung on a double string. Each delicate bead is separated by a small, light, topaz colored plastic bead. The necklace measures 7¾" with a 2¾" adjustable chain. Each clip earring is signed "GERMANY." 1940s. $115.00 – 145.00.

"Why do you build me up, buttercup baby?" says a song from the 1960s. This necklace is butter in color. Two strands of plastic beads, aurora borealis, molded plastic, and gold separators. Measures 11¾". Strung tightly, with no give. The clasp is gold tone. So striking! 1950s. $70.00 – 110.00.

People are seeing red for this beauty. Two strands of cranberry plastic beads are hand strung on cranberry colored string. Unsigned. Measures 9". 1940s to the early 1950s. $55.00 – 85.00.

Light brown, earthy tones make up this three-strand, 8½" necklace with a 3¼" adjustable chain. The plastic beads are separated by small aurora borealis beads that are tipped in gold tone. Signed "JAPAN." Late 1940s to the 1950s. $60.00 – 90.00.

What a vivid set! Three strands of green beads with aurora borealis and faux pearls separated by small beads. Strung on fish wire. Measures 6¼" with a 2¾" adjustable chain. Clip earrings to match. All pieces are weighted. Unmarked. Mid-1940s to the 1950s. $75.00 – 115.00.

Big, Bold, and Bulky

A 1950s beauty that measures 10½". Three beads, in series of three, are separated by small silver beads. The center, four fossil leaves are separated by three silver tubes. The necklace is made of wood and sterling. The colors are aqua with gold overlay, and silver serves to accent the fishhook clasp. This necklace is reversible. The back side of the leaves resemble feather paintings. Unsigned. $30.00 – 50.00.

Are you ready for the islands, "mahn"? A fishhook clasp to close this ebony and ivory 11" necklace. Glass beads. This piece reminds me of a piano. Lucite. Weighted. Unsigned. The five drops are mother of pearl with a black center stripe. Late 1930s to the early 1940s. $30.00 – 50.00.

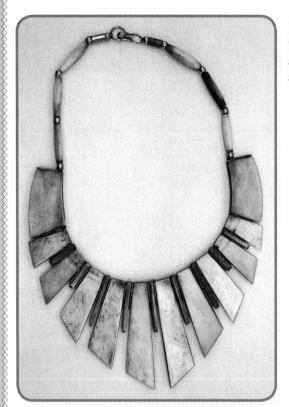

Beautiful in bone! Hand strung on string and flexible all the way. Unmarked. Measures 10". Made of bone, wood, and sterling. Late 1900s. The top has three long, tubular beads separated by small silver-tone beads. $40.00 – 80.00.

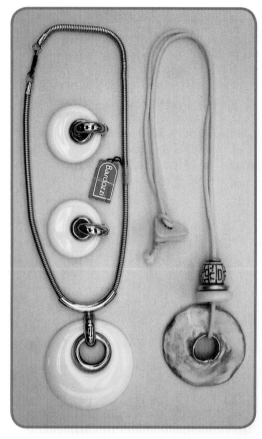

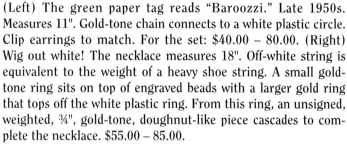

(Left) The green paper tag reads "Baroozzi." Late 1950s. Measures 11". Gold-tone chain connects to a white plastic circle. Clip earrings to match. For the set: $40.00 – 80.00. (Right) Wig out white! The necklace measures 18". Off-white string is equivalent to the weight of a heavy shoe string. A small gold-tone ring sits on top of engraved beads with a larger gold ring that tops off the white plastic ring. From this ring, an unsigned, weighted, ¾", gold-tone, doughnut-like piece cascades to complete the necklace. $55.00 – 85.00.

(Left) This azure assembly reminds me of the skies out west. 1970s, unsigned necklace. The beads are sterling and wood. Colors of corals, Santa Fe blues, and blacks are enameled over the copper base of the 3" wide drop. Matching pierced earrings measure 1½". $50.00 – 90.00. (Right) The 1970s counterpart to the Santa Fe necklace looks like something one might don to an event somewhere in the Four Corners region of our great United States. Unsigned. Necklace of plastic beads is done in corals, blacks, and aquas. The drop measures 3⅛" long and 2" wide. Enameled over copper. $45.00 – 85.00.

Show stopping! Four strands of black beads are hand strung on fish net. Each strand has a variety of colored beads to add flair to the black strands. Small silver beads on each strand are connected to the drop. Measures 12". The base measures 4" and is made of wood that is encased in leather. Matching pierced earrings. Late 1980s to the early 1990s. $65.00 – 105.00.

(Left) An artistic melody falls onto the drop of this necklace. Metal base is 3" of big browns with embossed gold tones in a scribble pattern. The silver and black beads are flat with round gold beads to separate. They measure 11¼" long. The necklace has a lobster claw clasp. 1970s. Unmarked. $50.00 – 90.00. (Right) Unsigned, 1970s necklace made of plastic beads. Matching pierced earrings are hand strung on string. Base measures 2½". Muted colors of grays, greens, browns, yellows, and three splashes of deep mauve. $45.00 – 85.00.

(Left) Buried treasure? No, it is a secret place to hide your signature scent. The concept of hiding things in jewelry began during the Renaissance when people sought to harm the regal. Early 1970s perfumer necklace. The back of the gold opens into a perfumer, which is comprised of plain brushed gold. 14" necklace. Unsigned. The faux earthy jade drop measures 2⅛". The front is a gold-tone, roped design with a gold bar to attach to the chain. $75.00 – 105.00. (Right) Brooch is 2¼", and it reminds me of the Southwest. Great colors. 1970s. Unsigned. $35.00 – 55.00.

A rose, by any other name, is still a rose. Shakespeare would have a ball with this floral fantasy. A lobster claw clasp secures this large gold beaded necklace. Unsigned. Measures 13". Matching clip earrings. The heart drop with the leaf is a nice finish for this bold set. 1970s. $55.00 – 85.00.

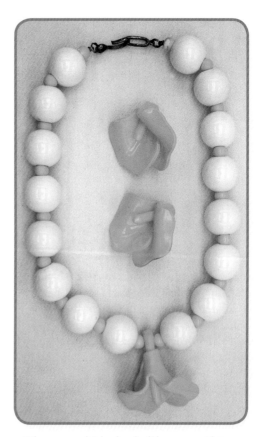

These orchids look like something that might be planted in a garden in Holland. Early 1950s, Lucite, small yellow, and large white beads with a lemon-colored flower center. Matching clip earrings measure 1¾". Unsigned. $40.00 – 80.00.

(Top) Weighty! Late 1940s to the early 1950s, racy red glass beads. Hand strung tightly on heavy white string. Unsigned. Measures 12". $40.00 – 70.00. (Bottom) At first glance, one might mistake this piece for gumballs. Big colorful beads are separated by flat gold spacers. Adjustable chain measures 3½", the necklace is 7". 1950s to the early 1960s. $45.00 – 85.00.

Trés boho! 1940s hand-crocheted necklace of six links and two balls. Four strands of hand-strung beads on fish wire are twisted. The links are green and bone colored. $45.00 – 75.00.

Calling all Jimmy Buffet fans: it is five o'clock somewhere! This puffy parrot is made from wood and hand painted. It is 5" in width. The red beads are hand strung on fishnet. Two gold flat discs separate the larger bottom beads. 1950s. Measures 12" long. $55.00 – 105.00.

(Left) Weighted! 9½" necklace. All hand strung. Five faux pearls on one side and six on the other side attach to two Lucite flowers colored with just a hint of pink. The beauty of this necklace with the 22 rows of small Lucite beads is remarkable. 1940s. $115.00 – 145.00. (Right) 9" clear white plastic beads with a fall of five feather-type fossil drops. Each is separated by two small gold-tone beads. Matching pierced earrings measure 2". 1950s. $55.00 – 85.00.

Christmas and Holiday

In the original box "Happy Holidays" bell from the late 1960s to the early 1970s sold at the discount stores. Examples are Murphy's, Woolworth's, McCory's. The top sprig of holly is enameled. $30.00 – 50.00.

(Left) Gather round the Christmas tree. A gold-tone Christmas tree pin from the 1960s to the early 1970s. Cabochons of green, red, and blue are sprinkled on the pine. This tree is topped with a blue star. Unsigned. The tree measures 2½". $40.00 – 80.00. (Center) These ornamental features are certain to light up the night. This tree is framed in a gold tone and holds enameled bulbs. Unsigned. Measures 2". This is from the 1960s – 1970s. Nice weight. $40.00 – 80.00. (Right) Signed "J.J." The 1960s – 1970s gold-tone tree is cut out. Strings in gold tone hold the bezel set stones. The star exudes a red center stone. Quality crafted. Measures 2¼". $55.00 – 85.00.

(Left) Ring-a-ling/hear them ring/soon it will be Christmas Day! Silver bells are signed "Gerry's." Measures 2¼". The top is completed in green enameling, and the bells are made of red cabochon. 1960s – 1970s. $60.00 – 90.00. (Right) Christmas time sweet! Candy cane pin is unsigned from the late 1960s to the mid-1970s. Enameled in red, green, and white over gold tone. Measures 2¼" long. $30.00 – 60.00.

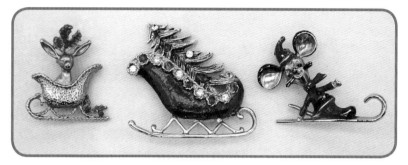

Janus 4" poinsettia pin. Five leaves in open gold tone have five small aurora borealis on the leaves. The center holds two leaves of red stones. One of each is done in garnet, red, and opalescent. 1970s – 1980s. Made well. $105.00 – 145.00.

(Left) You've heard of the Lone Ranger, now meet the Lone Reindeer. A gold-tone reindeer in a sleigh with green enameling for the holly and topped with a red berry. 1970s. Unmarked. $20.00 – 30.00. (Center) Signed "Hedy 1970s." Measures 1¾". Here comes the Christmas tree in the red enameled sleigh with a glamorous gold-tone runner. Red and white rhinestones are glued into the border of the sleigh. The green enameled tree has great pine detail with four small red and white stones. Measures 1¾". Quality. $55.00 – 95.00. (Right) Zooming down the hill! Signed "BJ." This enameled Christmas mouse is ready to sled! 1970s. $25.00 – 45.00.

May all your Christmases be white! Well, not quite, with these lovely, multi-colored tree pins. Both pins are from the late 1960s to the early 1970s. Each: $30.00 – 50.00.

(Left) Cute stocking pin. Gift boxes are crammed into the top of the boot while there are five green leaves and two faux seed pearls used for snow. Signed "Art." 1970s. 1½" long. $25.00 – 45.00. (Right) What a stocking stuffer and Christmas kitten! This gold-tone and red enameling pin has a kitten snug in a boot! The kitten's eyes are small, red rhinestones. 1960s. Unsigned. Measures 1½". $25.00 – 45.00.

(Left) This candle really burns bright! A tear-shaped red rhinestone is employed for the flame with a circle of gold for glow. White enameling makes the dripping wax; red enameling for the berries and green for the holly. Base has blue, yellow, red, and green glued stones. Late 1960s to the mid-1970s. It is signed, but the signature is illegible. $30.00 – 50.00. (Right) Another smart Christmas brooch. Three tear-shaped crystal flames with two golden glowing circles. Green and red enameling at the base with pine and a polished bow. Snow is flitted about the pin. Unsigned. Measures 1½". Late 1960s to the mid-1970s. $25.00 – 45.00.

(Left) Who wouldn't crave a cornucopia stuffed with gifts? Emerald leaves with multiple clear rhinestones and careful detailing to the presents. Measures 2¼". Signed "B.J." Late 1960s to the mid-1970s. $30.00 – 50.00. (Right) We want our packages delivered by this on-the-way sleigh! 1960s. $30.00 – 50.00.

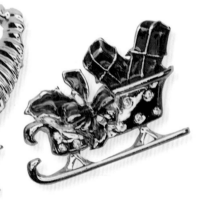

These swanky Christmas candles share many similarities. For starters, their bases are composed of gold toning. Neither candle is signed. Mid-1960s to the late 1960s. (Left) Measures 2". A crystal tear-shaped flame is glued in with white enameling for wax. An enameled sprig of holly holds berries. $25.00 – 45.00. (Right) Measures 1¾". A blue tear-shaped flame is glued in with a red enameled candle, hugged by a sprig of holly. $25.00 – 45.00.

(Left) A pretty wintergreen enameled, holly leaf pin. Measures 2½". Unsigned. Late 1960s. $25.00 – 45.00. (Right) Glued-in faux pearls drip from the gold-tone winter leaves. There are five small rhinestones on the piece and a glued-in, wintergreen stone at the base. 1960s. Unsigned. 2¼" long. $30.00 – 50.00.

(Left) This heavy, Christmas basket pin has evergreen-colored enameling for the basket. Nicely detailed, rope-styled handle. 1½". Unsigned. 1960s. $30.00 – 50.00. (Right) I wish this snowflake would fall on me! Five pairs of winter colored pierced earrings act as the wondrous colors of this perfect flake! 2¼". Looks like Avon. Late 1970s to the early 1980s. $20.00 – 40.00.

Christmas tree pin and pierced earrings set. Christmas gift boxes are stacked on this tree. Glued-on plastic beads and a star top the tree. Tree measures 2¾" long, earrings are 1" long. Set was in the original Avon box. Late 1970s to the early 1980s. $20.00 – 30.00.

Silver-tone hinged bracelet with excellent detail! 1960s. Cute earrings. Rhinestones are scattered on the snowy white earrings. For the set: $110.00 – 150.00.

Nice necklace and marvelous matching clip earrings. The earrings are made of a large bead suspended from a small bead. Two strands of red, plastic beads are strung on red strings to make the necklace. Finishes with a large, fishhook clasp. Measures 6½". Early 1950s. Unsigned. $30.00 – 60.00.

(Left) Oh! Christmas tree, how lovely are your branches! Gold wash over plating with small green, blue, citrine, and red rhinestones embedded. Rhinestones are in groups of four on ten places on the tree. A citrine is used for the star. 2½". Unsigned. $50.00 – 100.00. (Right) A sturdy Christmas tree pin on gold wash plating. An amalgam of colored stones are glued into the pin, and there are etched stones for the background. 2¼" long. 1950s to the 1960s. Unsigned. $50.00 – 100.00.

(Left) Green over gold for the pin with six gold balls and a star on the top. 2". Unsigned. 1960s. $30.00 – 60.00. (Center) Sharply defined pines with small green, white, red, and blue rhinestones. One stone is missing on the bottom right. A finished pot with gold rivets. 2¼". 1950s to the 1960s. Unsigned. $40.00 – 70.00. (Right) Christmas-y rhinestones in white, red, and green. A green, pear-shaped stone tops the tree. Nice quality. 1¾". Early 1960s. $50.00 – 105.00.

(Left) Rocking wreath! Laden with silver-tone holly leaves and gold berries. 1½". 1960s. Unsigned. $50.00 – 100.00. (Right) Silver tone with Christmas green and red enameling. Three goldish pine cones and silvery red berries. Christmas cute! Late 1950s. 1½". Unsigned. $40.00 – 70.00.

(Left) Plastic wreath with pine green holly and red berries. A bow finishes the piece. 1¾". 1950s. Unsigned. $35.00 – 65.00. (Right) Quality green and white rhinestones with a gold bow on the top and a center red stone. 1¼". Not signed; I am in shock about this! Early 1960s. $55.00 – 100.00.

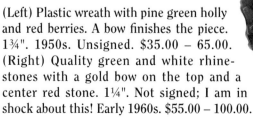

(Left) Pierced bell earrings. A gold bell with light metal ribbon in red, green, and gold that is suspended from a red, satin rope. 2¼". 1970s. Unsigned. $15.00 – 35.00. (Center) Better than your average bell pin. A red, enameled ribbon with a drop of three chains holding each bell. Rather flexible. 2¼" long. 1950s. Unsigned. $20.00 – 40.00. (Right) Silver tone with green and red enameling bell pin. A bow is used to top. Super cute! 1¼". 1960s. Unsigned. $30.00 – 50.00.

(Left) Unique and cool guitar gift pin. Has three holly leaves with berries and a ribbon. A coat charm is suspended from the side. 1950s. 3". $30.00 – 60.00. (Right) Lovely holly pin made of gold plating. Very heavy with enameling. Six red berries are raised from the leaf. Pavé rhinestones complete the top. 2". Early to mid-1960s. Unsigned. $45.00 – 85.00.

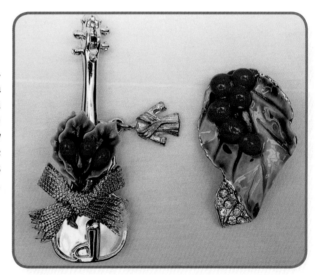

(Top left) Pierced poinsettia earrings. Unsigned, but looks like Avon. 1970s. $15.00 – 35.00. (Bottom left) Winter white poinsettia pin converts to a necklace. How clever! Unsigned, but looks like Avon. 1970s. $20.00 – 50.00. (Top right) Clip earrings. (Bottom right) Pierced earrings. Both pairs are unsigned, but look like Avon. 1970s. $15.00 – 35.00.

(Left) A rocking reindeer tac pin! Gold tone with a hint of red for the bridle. Signed "Avon." 1970s. $15.00 – 25.00. (Right) Highly detailed reindeer pins with bright red Rudolph noses. Gold with Christmas colors for the enameling and poinsettias used as bows. The reindeer on the right is still in the original package. 1¾". Unsigned. 1970s. $30.00 – 60.00.

(Left) Chic candlestick with white enameled body. Wax is dripping because the candle burns so hot! Red rhinestones are laced through the enameled pine needles. 2¼". Unsigned. 1960s. $30.00 – 50.00. (Right) Cuddly Mr. and Mrs. Snowman pin! A cozy, warm, creative pin set in a silver frame. The picture says it all. Back is silver. 1¾". 1950s. Unsigned. $55.00 – 85.00.

(Top) Santa pin and pierced earrings set. Chalk-like base with paint. 1¼" earrings, the pin measures one inch more. Early 1970s. Set: $20.00 – 40.00. (Bottom) Snowman pin and pierced earrings set. Chalk-like base and paint. Unsigned. $40.00 – 60.00.

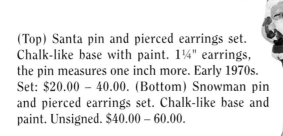

(Left) Christmas angels. 1¾". Signed on the gold tag, "Made in China." Mid-1970s. $15.00 – 30.00. (Right) Pierced earrings and necklace set. Gold bells are suspended from a red, satin cord. Low budget. 16¾", necklace; 2¼", earrings. Unsigned. 1970s. For the set: $20.00 – 40.00.

(Left) Glued-in red stones with a white stone on the side. Three holly leaves are enameled and hold the two berries. 1¼" long. Signed "Avon" on both earrings. 1970s. $15.00 – 20.00. (Center) Santa cat pin. A fish is suspended from the link on his collar. Silver-tone face, ears, and tassel. Black enameled eye and nose with gold whiskers, collar, and outline of the red painted Santa hat. 2¼". 1970s. Marked "49088." $25.00 – 55.00. (Right) Gold-tone ribbon with enameled poinsettias and a gold-tone, beaded pine cone. Signed "Taiwan." 1¾". 1970s. $20.00 – 40.00.

(Left) Oh, the weather outside is frightful, but this pin is so delightful! This Christmas inspired wreath brooch has a red rhinestone glued in on the top of the bell. Small red, blue, and green cabochons are scattered about the leaves of the pin, with white enameling for the snow. 1¾" diameter. Unsigned. 1960s. $50.00 – 80.00. (Right) And since we've no place to go, let it snow, let it snow, let it snow! You'll be begging for snow when you wear this pin. This weighty pin has peridot topaz rhinestones and ruby cabochons splayed on the pin. Red, green, and white enameling complete the pin, and a red bow with a red center rhinestone is perched from the top. 1960s. $50.00 – 80.00.

(Left) Gold-tone plating with red enameled bow with gold, green, and red enameled beads surrounding the ringing bell, which is a small faux pearl. 1¾". Unsigned. 1960s. $45.00 – 75.00. (Center) Circle sprig of winter. Gold-tone plating. The gold circle embraces the sprig of emerald-colored rhinestones and a bow of small faux pearls. At the ends you will find a pea green rhinestone. 1¾". Unmarked. Early 1960s. $40.00 – 50.00. (Right) The Christmas wreath pin has gold-tone plating and is very heavy. There are three rows of holly with green and red enameled berries, also green enameling on the ribbon. 1½". Signed "GERRYS©." 1960s. $60.00 – 80.00.

You'll go gaga over these Christmas pins! (Left) Gold-tone plating. Christmas green rhinestones glued in with small red rhinestones. In the center, a gold bow to top with center red rhinestone. 1½". Signed "WEISS." 1960s. $90.00 – 130.00. (Center) Small Christmas wreath. Green enameled wreath with silver and red enameled beads. Bottom bow boasts red enameling and a silver bead center. 1". Unmarked. Early 1960s. $35.00 – 55.00. (Right) Christmas wreath. Weighted nice for a coat. Green and red enameling for pine and holly. A candle burns bright with a citrine-colored rhinestone. 2" wide. Unsigned. 1960s. $50.00 – 80.00.

Rockin' around the Christmas trees! (Left) Gold-tone plating. Small red and green rhinestones decorate this tree. Red and green beads for tinsel, and an enameled star on top with a red rhinestone center. 1¾". Unmarked. 1960s. $45.00 – 65.00. (Center) I love this one! This pin is gold-tone plating. It's weighted and would look perfect on a heavy blazer. Glued-in stones for ornaments have open foiled backing. Small seed beads for trim. 2½". Unmarked. 1960s. $80.00 – 110.00. (Right) Gold-tone plating. Silver tone over the gold tree for a great tinsel look! Small red, green, and purple cabochons for the tree ornaments, topped off with a small green rhinestone. 2". Unsigned. 1960. $45.00 – 65.00.

These svelte pieces would drive any woman wild. (Left) Christmas tree pin. Gold-tone plating. Reminds me of a simple true Christmas. Glued-in rhinestones for ornaments. A gold tree trunk and pot. 2¼". Unsigned. $20.00 – 30.00. (Right) An Avon Christmas tree pin, measures 2¼" long. The six gold electroplated bows have centers of aurora borealis stones. $40.00 – 80.00.

(Left) Christmas tree pin with red and green enameling for pine and ornaments, with open pines. A red enameled pot to finish. 2¼". Unsigned. 1960s to the 1970s. $40.00 – 60.00. (Center) A gold-tone plated Christmas tree pin with white enameling for snow. Green enameling is for the pine with three red enameled candy canes. The star topper includes a red rhinestone. 2½". Signed "©BJ." 1960s to the 1970s. $45.00 – 65.00. (Right) A weighty Christmas tree pin. Gold-tone plating. Green enameling and red for the ornaments topped off with a red enameled star. 2¼". ©BEATRIX. $40.00 – 60.00.

(Left) This bell brooch is quite weighty. Gold-tone plating. Multicolored stones, glued-in green leaves that are detailed with small red stones, and one red stone on the ringer. "©BEATRIX." $90.00 – 130.00. (Right) This bell brooch is gold-tone plating. Christmas red and green over the silver-tone bells, with small pavé rhinestones for bell base and silver for the ringer. 2¼". Unsigned. $70.00 – 110.00.

Ring my bell, ring my bell! (Left) Gold-tone plating. This bell really rings! Green enameled leaves with a red cabochon. Holly tops off the bell. 1½". Unmarked. 1960s to early 1970s. $40.00 – 70.00. (Center) Gold-tone plating, and it really jingles, too! 2". Unmarked. 1960s. $45.00 – 75.00. (Right) Gold-tone plating. Dark green and red molded plastic for the holly trim. 1½" wide. Unmarked. Early 1970s. $30.00 – 50.00.

(Left) Candle pin of the 1960s. Ruby flame with white enameling for the wax. Base of gold with detailed holly and pine. 1½" long and 1¾" wide. $30.00 – 50.00. (Center) 2½" candle. Nice detail with the colors of the enameling. Small red rhinestones with one aurora borealis in the pine. 1960s. $30.00 – 50.00. (Right) 1¾", 1960s candle pin. Three pear-shaped ruby flames with a gold-tone base that has enameling for the wax and pine detail. All three of these are unsigned. Weighted. $30.00 – 50.00.

Indiana, Pennsylvania, is the Christmas tree capital of the world. (Left) 2¼" Christmas tree pin of the 1950s. Gold tone with colored stones for ornaments. Unsigned. $20.00 – 40.00. (Center) Beatrix Christmas tree pin is 2½". Pin signed under the closure. Enameled over the gold tone in Christmas colors. Simple yet classic. 1960s. $30.00 – 50.00. (Right) 2½" Christmas tree pin is unsigned. This would be pretty on a coat. It is weighted. Pine is in 3-D with colored stones for the bulbs. $20.00 – 40.00.

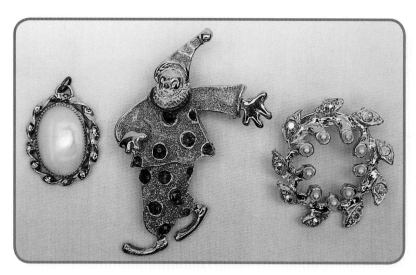

(Left) Winter white pendant. 1" oval in a bezel setting. A delicate swirl border. Open backed. Unsigned. $50.00 – 80.00. (Center) Clown pin measures 2¼". Flexible bottom as this clown makes his moves. Gold-tone top with colored stones. Bottom is silver tone with colored stones. Shoes, hands, and face are gold tone. Red enameled collar. Unsigned. $45.00 – 75.00. (Right) Rockin' wreath of aurora borealis and seed pearls. 1960s. $25.00 – 45.00.

Screw-on earrings. Christmas bells. Two purple plastic beads are in the center of the bell. 1940s. Unsigned. $15.00 – 20.00.

(Left) Pin. Snow covered bells with pink beads in the center dangle from the Christmas bow. Dainty. Unsigned. 1940s. $10.00 – 15.00. (Right) Gold-tone bells, enameled red ringers, and green ivy. 1950s. $15.00 – 25.00.

Ringing in the season! (Left) Silver bells! Silver bells! These silver bells ring. They are suspended from the holly. In the center of the pine and holly is a red cabochon berry. Unsigned. Measures 2⅛". Pin from the 1950s. $25.00 – 45.00. (Right) Golden Christmas bell rings with the ringer. Berry and holly are enameled. 2". Pin is unsigned. 1950s. $20.00 – 30.00.

(Left) Poinsettia wreath pin from the 1960s. Enameling over metal. $25.00 – 45.00. (Right) This poinsettia Christmas pin is from the mid-1950s to the early 1960s. $35.00 – 55.00.

(Top) This bracelet is fun with all its Christmas fruit. 1960s. $30.00 – 50.00. (Bottom) Avon bracelet from the 1970s that slides. $25.00 – 45.00.

Cu Later Copper

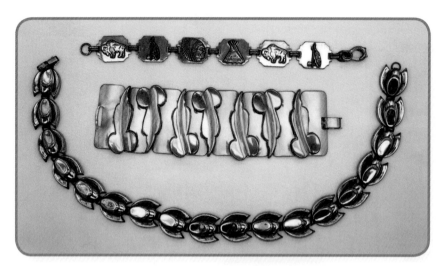

(Top) Bracelet measures 6½". Unmarked. Raised Indian scenes on each panel link. $30.00 – 50.00. (Center) Renoir copper bracelet that measures 5¾". Weighty. $50.00 – 80.00. (Bottom) This necklace measures 14½" and is unmarked. $45.00 – 65.00.

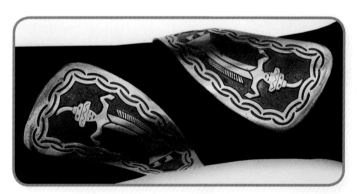

This hinged bracelet is signed twice "Jar Solid Copper." $70.00 – 100.00.

(Left) This cuff bracelet has a rope design and is weighty. Unsigned. $55.00 – 75.00. (Center) Matisse Renoir bracelet. $70.00 – 110.00. (Right) Hinged bracelet that is unmarked. Has three leaves on each side. $45.00 – 75.00.

Not copper, however, it fits quite nicely in this chapter because of its appearance. 1¾" stone in bracelet is set on a closed backing. The stone in the ring measures 1⅛". Both are dark topaz colored and bezel set. They are made of brass. Weighty. Mid 1940s to the early 1950s. $105.00 – 125.00 each.

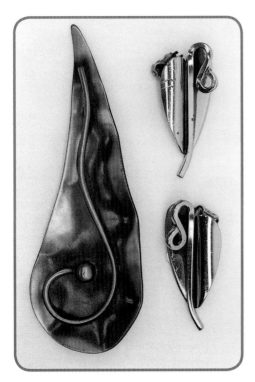

"There Is No Arizona." Remember the song? Southwest design for this unsigned copper necklace. The pendant measures 2" with the chain at 14¾". 1950s. $85.00 – 110.00.

(Left) Brooch is signed "GENUINE COPPER." Mid-1940s to the early 1950s. Measures 3¾". $100.00 – 130.00. (Right) Each of the clip earrings is signed "Renoir." Measures 1½". 1940s. $60.00 – 80.00.

This copper pin converts to a pendant with matching screw-back earrings. The pin is weighted. It measures 1¾" with the earrings ¾". Each piece is signed "Renoir." Mid-1940s to the early 1950s. Earrings $70.00 – 100.00. Pin $80.00 – 120.00.

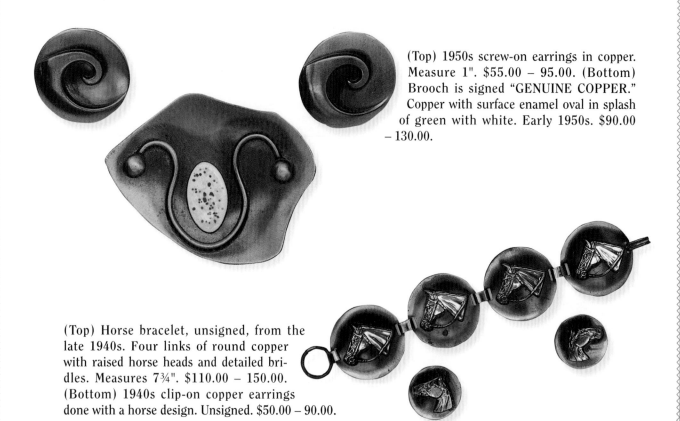

(Top) 1950s screw-on earrings in copper. Measure 1". $55.00 – 95.00. (Bottom) Brooch is signed "GENUINE COPPER." Copper with surface enamel oval in splash of green with white. Early 1950s. $90.00 – 130.00.

(Top) Horse bracelet, unsigned, from the late 1940s. Four links of round copper with raised horse heads and detailed bridles. Measures 7¾". $110.00 – 150.00. (Bottom) 1940s clip-on copper earrings done with a horse design. Unsigned. $50.00 – 90.00.

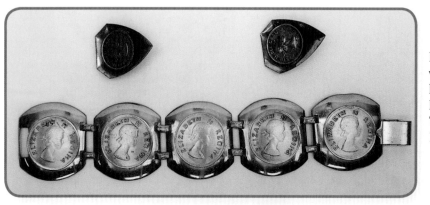

Bracelet and clip earrings that are weighted. This lovely copper bracelet has four links in two rows holding the Elizabeth II Regina coins. Measures 7¼". Matching earrings measure 1¼". 1940s. $110.00 – 150.00 set.

(Top) 7⅛" copper bracelet with seven rectangle links done in a Southwest design. Mid-1940s to the mid-1950s. $85.00 – 125.00. (Bottom) Ride 'em, cowgirl! A 7" copper bracelet with eight links in a design of a cowboy hat. Unsigned. Mid-1940s to the mid-1950s. $85.00 – 125.00.

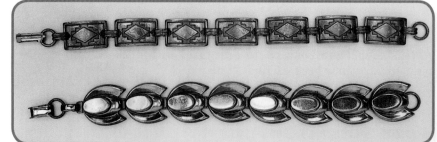

Looks like fall for all of these copper clip earrings. Mid-1940s to the mid-1950s. Each pair of earrings is detailed, showing quality craftsmanship. (Top) Measures 1¾". (Center) Measures 1¼". (Bottom) Measures 1¼". All pairs valued at $65.00 – 105.00.

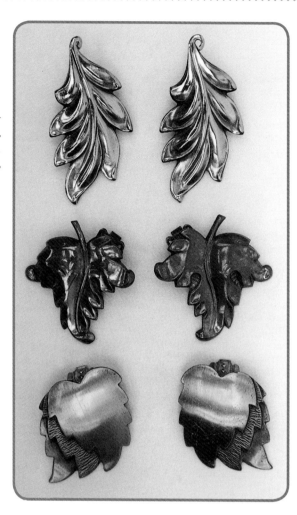

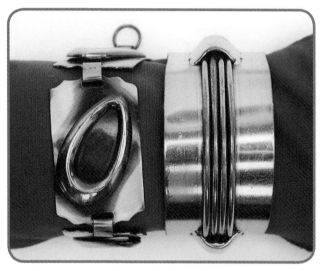

(Left) Super swirls. Unsigned. Copper. 1950s. $80.00 – 105.00. (Right) Cuff bracelet from the 1950s. Copper. Unsigned. $90.00 – 105.00.

1950s unsigned copper earrings. Measure 1½". The ¾" emerald stone is held by four prongs. $50.00 – 80.00.

Flower Power

Every botanist's dream. This 3½" crimson flower has very pointy petals. Six petals overlap the other six petals. The center is a burnt orange color. Unmarked. 1960s. $25.00 – 45.00.

These double trouble flowers measure 3½". 1960s. Unmarked. Outrageously orange and radiantly red, the enameled flower petals are not only pointed, but they literally jag you when touched. $30.00 – 50.00.

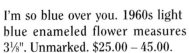

Paint the town red in this remarkable pin! Unmarked, 1960s, flower pin. Measures 2". Heavily enameled in a duller orange color. 3-D effect. $15.00 – 25.00.

I'm so blue over you. 1960s light blue enameled flower measures 3⅛". Unmarked. $25.00 – 45.00.

Faded glory. Two toned, blue tipped with the petals tipped in white. The center is an aurora borealis. 1960s. Unmarked. $15.00 – 25.00.

I have never seen a purple and black flower, though if it does exist in nature, it's surely stunning. The three rows of lightweight metal petals raise upwards. A nice tough to the center done in dark purple rhinestones. Late 1960s early 1970s. Unsigned. Measures 2¼". $20.00 – 40.00.

This peony reminds me of late night dancing in the streets during Carnival season. Late 1960s early 1970s. Measures 3¼". Unmarked. This weighty pin has great detailing. The leaves are black with green enameling. Six petals in deep purple are tipped with black. The center holds five small, pea green rhinestones. Unmarked. $20.00 – 40.00.

Springtime delight! Weighted metal. Late 1960s. Unmarked. The back is done in gold electroplate. Four swirling petals in a lilac color make this flower delectable. The center holds white faux pearls and is sprinkled with seven small rhinestones. Nicely crafted. $20.00 – 40.00.

Go Pittsburgh Steelers! This 3¼" black and gold flower is bursting with excitement. The first row of petals are enameled in black. The top layer is gold. The gold petals were brushed and sprinkled with more gold to give the look of dew. Late 1960s to the early 1970s. Unmarked. $35.00 – 55.00.

Full bloomin' beauty! 3⅛" unsigned metal gold flower. Two tones of gold and two rows of petals done in 3-D. The center is button like done in gold to match the first row of petals. 1960s. $30.00 – 50.00.

Rainy nights in Georgia/Kentucky rain/here comes that rainy day feeling again. Gary Allen wrote *Songs about Rain*, but this pin captures the emotions of rain with its dismal gray in high gloss enameling. Two rows of large petals in gray and black. The first row is black and the second is lighter silver gray. The top row is made of small silver petals with a black center. Unmarked. 1960s. $25.00 – 55.00.

2¾", late 1960s pin. This pin converts to a pendant. The six petals are done in a screen-like fashion. Bordered by a silver-tone frame. The center is button like. A screen framed in a silver-tone ring. Completely unique. Measures 2¾". Unmarked. $25.00 – 45.00.

1960s silver-tone pin is unsigned. Measures 2½".
Short stemmed. Silver-tone flower is framed with
a roping of silver tone. The petals are a solid silver-
tone color. The center holds a lone aurora borelias
stone. Unsigned. Weighted. $20.00 – 30.00.

Unsigned 2¾" gold-tone pin. Done in 3-D. 1960s, gracious gold
flower pin with a faux pearl center. The pearl sits down in a
shallow cup encompassed with small gold beads. 1960s. $15.00
– 25.00.

Measures 2½". The back is brushed gold. Six wowing white
petals are raised. Three gold-tone petals hug the three white
petals with a gray faux pearl set inside the petals. Would be
pretty worn in the winter season. Weighted and well crafted.
1960s. $30.00 – 50.00.

Signed "© COVENTRY" backing is silver tone. This flower is
heavy. The white cabochons are opened back. They are bordered by a silver-tone rope design. Each petal is separated with
a silver-tone bar. The center cabochon is round. Late 1960s to
the early 1970s. $35.00 – 55.00.

Unsigned 2½" warm white petals are tipped in a brushed black enameling. The second row of petals is raised off the first row. The center is small. I am surprised this is so light weight. 1960s. $15.00 – 30.00.

I have never seen petals shaped like this! They are really in a swirl. The white enameled petals are raised. The center is black and looks to be finished like a beehive. Unmarked. 1960s. Measures 2½". $15.00 – 25.00.

2½" round and 1" deep. Basic black and wonderfully white. Unsigned. The enameling is high gloss. Well crafted. 1960s. $25.00 – 45.00.

How heavy! This flower pin converts to a pendant. The base of the back is a gold-tone circle to support the petals. Wildly white petals in a variety of sizes. The center is gold tone. Unmarked. 1960s. $20.00 – 30.00.

Jagalicious lemon zest and garden green flower! 3¼"
1960s flower pin. Lemon and grass colors flow from
these petals. The center seed is rough enameling.
Unsigned. $25.00 – 35.00.

They call it mellow yellow. A nicely done daisy. Petals are
set in an every other pattern. The center is flat. Unsigned.
Measures 2½". Late 1960s – early 1970s. $15.00 – 25.00.

Butterlicious. Flower pin measures 3½". 1960s. Unsigned.
Four large petals with a nice yolk colored center. The stem is
enameled in green. $30.00 – 50.00.

Measures 2" and is deep with five petals in the first and second
rows. The center is done in gold-tone sprigs tipped in small
rhinestones holding a center faux pearl. 1960s. Weighted. $30.00
– 60.00.

1960s. Measures 2½". Unsigned. Pale yellow. Two rows of lightweight petals hold the raised center. $20.00 – 30.00.

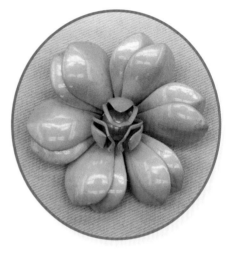

Two's company, too! A series of six petals in twos. The center is raised. Measures 2½". 1960s. Unmarked. $20.00 – 40.00.

Stamped "©SARAH COV." Measures 3¼". Late 1960s to the early 1970s. Two-tone grassy green petals for the base. These petals are jagged. The gold-tone petals set down in the green. The center also is gold. $30.00 – 50.00.

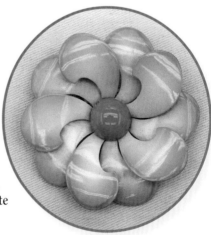

This creme de menthe green flower pin measures 2½". A swirling pattern of five petals with every other petal being raised. 1960s. Unsigned. Unmarked. The back is white enameling. $20.00 – 40.00.

A stretchy sunburst of color. 2¾" flower pin from the 1960s. It is unsigned. Enameled metal petals are done in green and white. Center is green. $20.00 – 30.00.

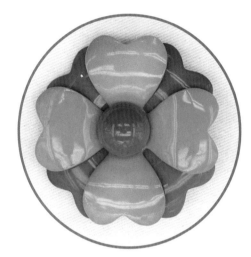

The heart shaped petals are in two-tone green, the back is done in white. Nice weight. 1960s to the early 1970s. Unmarked. 2⅛". $15.00 – 25.00.

These light coral colored petals are set in fives. The top row is raised off the bottom. A small flower in the center has a small mother of pearl center. The back is white. 1960s to the early 1970s. Unsigned. Measures 3". $25.00 – 45.00.

Unsigned 2½" flower pin. Jagged tipped petals. Taupe and burnt orange enameling. Backing is finished in silver tone. 1960s. $20.00 – 40.00.

This metal flower pin's back is pink. Measures 2⅛". Pastel salmon colored petals. The seeds in the center are coral colored. Unmarked. 1960s. $15.00 – 20.00.

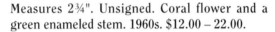

Measures 2¾". Unsigned. Coral flower and a green enameled stem. 1960s. $12.00 – 22.00.

The petals on this flower are raised and look like the color of butter. Grass green enameled stem with a leaf on each side. The back is enameled. 1960s, unmarked. 3". $20.00 – 30.00.

3¾", 1960s unsigned flower pin. Bright coral colored petals on this flower. The stem is enameled in a light green as are the leaves. The back is enameled. $20.00 – 30.00.

All are unsigned. All are from the 1960s. (Left) Simple flower pin in burnt orange with a stem of green. Measures 2¼". $10.00 – 15.00. (Center) Citrus colors for the lone flower. $8.00 – 16.00. (Right) Gold-tone stem and a flower done in orange enameling. Backing is gold tone. Measures 2¼". $8.00 – 12.00.

Both are from the 1960s and they are unmarked. (Left) Measures 3½". White heart-shaped petals on this daisy mae. A long enameled stem. $12.00 – 22.00. (Right) Pretty pastel enameled colors cover the petals of the flower. Five silver tipped petals are the base of this pretty. $12.00 – 22.00.

Both are unmarked. 1960s. (Left) Purple daisy measures 3½". Green enameled stem. $20.00 – 25.00. (Right) The back is the same color as the flower. The five petals are brushed in a darker green. $20.00 – 25.00.

Both are early 1970s, and unmarked. (Left) Backing is open gold-tone filigree. The flower buds are blue, coral, and pink. The leaves on the base are green. $25.00 – 35.00. (Right) Lemon yellow petals are raised with center seeds that are set in the petals. The stem is enameled brown and the leaf is green. The back of the leaf and stem is painted white. $25.00 – 35.00.

(Left) Still on the original jewelry card tag. Daisy pin with matching clip earrings. The bottom of the card reads "D DuBARRY F/A." Enameled pine green with royal blue centers. 1960s. $15.00 – 25.00. (Right) 2⅛" Signed "TRIFARI C" weighted flower pin. The back is gold wash over metal. The flower is enameled in blue with gold-tone accents and center. 1960s to the early 1970s. $20.00 – 25.00.

(Left) 3½" long. This Japanese rose is enameled in pink with three black sprigs. The tips are finished in six small pink rhinestones. Unsigned. 1960s. $15.00 – 20.00. (Right) A yellow rose with green enameling for the leaves. 1960s. Unsigned. Measures 2½". $15.00 – 20.00.

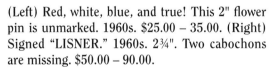

(Left) Measures 2½". 1960s. Six large petals in pink tipped in black enameling. The center is a large raised purple-pink dotted enameled. Fun pin. $20.00 – 30.00. (Right) Small unmarked pin of the 1960s. The leaves compose the base and are enameled in green. The first row of petals are deep red. The top row is hot pink. $10.00 – 15.00.

(Left) Red, white, blue, and true! This 2" flower pin is unmarked. 1960s. $25.00 – 35.00. (Right) Signed "LISNER." 1960s. 2¾". Two cabochons are missing. $50.00 – 90.00.

All pins are unmarked. (Top) Bumblebees are buzzing. Nice scatter pins. $25.00 – 35.00. (Center) A set of scatter pins done in butterflies. I would like to see these in my garden. Pavé rhinestones to cover. Done in silver tone. (Bottom Row) Each is unmarked and from the late 1960s to the early 1970s. (Bottom left) Gold tone shows the aurora borealis stone. The spine is faux pearls. The eyes are very small ruby colored glass. $15.00 – 20.00. (Bottom right) Mother of pearl winged butterfly. $15.00 – 25.00.

1960s. Unsigned flower pin in gold tone. $20.00 – 30.00.

This gorgeous gaggle of greens is from the 1960s. All pins are unmarked. Each: $20.00 – 30.00.

(Left) Five yellow petals with jagged edges. The center consists of five burnt orange petals that are raised so the seeds sink into the center. The stem is green with a detailed leaf on each side. Unmarked. 1960s. $25.00 – 35.00. (Center) This brown-eyed Susan has six pale yellow seeds raised off the petals. The stem is green with a leaf on each side. Measures 4⅛". 1960s. Unsigned. $25.00 – 35.00. (Right) 2½" of a cluster of four yellow daisies with orange centers. There is a raised ribbon over the green stem. $12.00 – 17.00.

All pieces are from the 1960s. (Left) 3¼". The back of this flower is gold metal. Five orange petals are tipped with black. The center is pea green with the three leafs to match. $15.00 – 20.00. (Center) Five pink petals with five purple petals hugging the opal pink center. The stem is green. Unsigned. Measures 4". 1960s. $25.00 – 35.00. (Right) Two sets of five burnt red petals are raised. The ends are tipped in black. The center is made of red glass cabochons set in shallow cups. Measures 2¾". $25.00 – 35.00.

All pins are from the 1960s and are unsigned. (Left) Two daisies with seven small daisies set on the white stem with a lone green leaf. The back is finished in white enameling. $8.00 – 10.00. (Center) 3¼" bursting with sunshine are the large petals in white and green. The center is 1" and orange. $20.00 – 25.00. (Right) The daisy is 4". Truly a daisy that grows in the yard. The three leafs are done in green enameling and are detailed. $25.00 – 35.00.

Glitzy Gold

(Left to right) This pretty necklace measures 14". Early 1970s. The pear-shaped brown stones measure 1". The pendant is opened backed, and the back is etched heavily. The inside is signed "Goldette." A barrel clasp to close. $80.00 – 120.00. 1970s gold-tone chain measures 7½", the drop measures 2½". Unsigned. A fun design on this weighted drop. $70.00 – 110.00. Chain measures 13½", the pendant measures 2½". Early 1970s. Unmarked. The open back oval citrine measures 1". Weighty. Nice quality necklace. $135.00 – 175.00. Measures 11¾". Unmarked. 1970s. Citrine is bezel set and open backed. Weighty. $110.00 – 130.00.

(Left) Holy owl! The owl measures 4¼" and the chain is 12". From the 1970s and unsigned. The eyes are made of small gold balls attached to two small chains so they have movement. $80.00 – 120.00. (Right) Measures 14½". This would be great on any Republican first ladies! Stamped on the lower left backside of the elephant ear reads "©SIR – R." The ears are gold electroplate and the face is weighted plastic. 1970s to the early 1980s. $100.00 – 140.00.

(Left) This necklace's filigree work is outstanding! It measures 9" with the longer adjustable chain measuring 5", the other chain with the fishhook clasp measures 2½". The amethyst stones are opened back. This looks as though it could be from West Germany. It is not signed. 1950s. $170.00 – 240.00. (Right) 1950s, signed "W. GERMANY," measures 15". The filigree work linked to the chain is in a series of three attached to faux pearls which are attached to a heart. The drop is weighty. Blue cabochons surround the two small pearls on each side of the bezel set center. The backing is done in heavy filigree. $170.00 – 240.00.

(Left) Stamped on the back in a gold-tone bar "CELEBRITY N.Y." Measures 13¼". A gold clasp attaches to the faux jade center. 1970s to early 1980s. $75.00 – 115.00. (Center) Unsigned 1970s necklace chain. Measures 13". The drop is 3½". Twelve small emeralds border the antiqued gold-tone drop. The oval cabochon is bordered by the marcisite. Opened back. $115.00 – 145.00. (Right) Signed "W. GERMANY," from the 1950s, and measures 14½". The center emerald colored stone is 1" and opened backed. Two sizes of emerald stones are bezel set on the frame of the necklace. Sizable, but delicate. $160.00 – 230.00.

(Top left) Unsigned 1¾" bird that looks like it should be signed Spain. (Top Right) Stamped "Spain," 2". Each has nice detail. Each: $30.00 – 70.00. (Center) 7" bracelet looks like it should be signed Spain, but it is not. 1950s. Gold tone with four rows of links that are etched in black. The five rows of gold-tone links border the bracelet. $70.00 – 105.00. (Bottom) Unmarked unusual gold-tone bracelet with a huge molded plastic stone for the center. It is set in four prongs. Two rows of gold-tone links hold the large center. Late 1970s. $70.00 – 120.00.

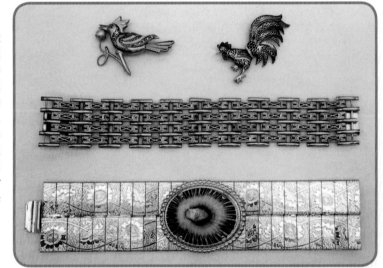

A pastiche of colors and textures form this 3" butterfly, which has beautiful colors. The cabochons look rich on the gold tone with the pavé stones. Weighty. 1970s. Unmarked. $75.00 – 105.00.

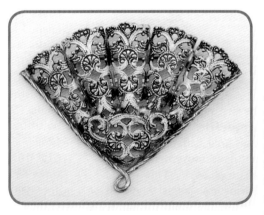

This 1960s fan is 3" at the widest area. Looks like it could be from Spain and disguise those Spanish eyes; it is not signed, though. Intricate work in the gold, silver, and black filigree. The gold-tone rope bordering the fan finishes it well. $90.00 – 130.00.

A regal pin resembling the colors of the crown. 1970s, round gold-tone brooch with faux pearls, multi-colored stones in three colors. Reminds me of royalty. 2" round, nice weight. Unmarked. $70.00 – 105.00.

Good to go green. 2½" round, antiqued gold-tone brooch shows the faux jade cabochons with a relaxed look. Late 1960s, unmarked. $70.00 – 105.00.

1¾" round antiqued gold-tone pin with seven faux pearls and three emerald stones at the base; the drop is flexible. The center faux jade is set in dog teeth. Nice craftsmanship. Weighted. Late 1960s. $85.00 – 135.00.

(Left) 1970s unsigned brooch. Unique gold tone with a light salmon cabochon to the right. Two aurora borealis stones hug the center pearl. Five flexible chains dangle with a faux pearl to finish. $65.00 – 95.00. (Right) 2¼" gold-tone pin looks like it is signed "Coro," hard to read the signature. The leaf holds the spray of faux pearls. The four leaves are a rough texture. Simple, yet pretty. 1970s. $80.00 – 120.00.

Cupid is ready to strike and engage young lovers in amorous adventures. The border is done in gold tone with a light citrine glass etched with cupids. Converts from a brooch to a pendant. 1960s. $90.00 – 140.00.

A lovely leaf that fell from a whispering tree somewhere in the great gold forest. Unmarked gold-tone leaf from the 1970s. This should be signed. It is heavy. 2¾". $60.00 – 90.00.

(Left) Here kitty kitty. Gold-tone cat with pavé rhinestones. Emeralds for the eyes. A green cabochon for the cat's hips. 1970s. $55.00 – 85.00. (Right) Signed "Roman," from the 1970s. This lady bug has onyx enameling with rhinestones set in the gold-tone body. Ruby enameling dots the bug. $50.00 – 80.00.

(Left) Jumping Johnny! 1970s gold-tone frog with green enameled spots. Onyx colored eyes. Signed "©Ron." $50.00 – 80.00. (Center) Wahoo fish. 1970s gold-tone fish. Nice pavé stones finish the facial area. The emerald eye sparkles. Etched gold-tone scales. Nice fins. The backing is open filigree. Weighted. Should be signed but it is not. $65.00 – 85.00. (Right) Tickled by turtles. Signed "Gerry's." 1970s turtle in antiqued gold tone with a detailed shell. The eyes are small rubies. $55.00 – 85.00.

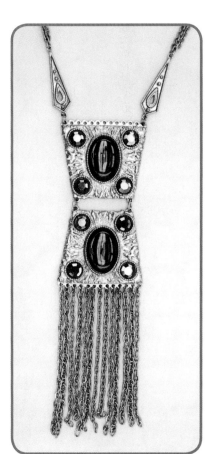

The necklace is unsigned. It measures 20", and each side has three chains connecting to a sleek 1¼" bar in a series of two. Four smaller amethyst cabochons with the larger center oval cabochon done in a series of two. The gold-tone drop is 7". Thirteen flexible chains dangle from the necklace. 1970s. $135.00 – 175.00.

(Bottom) Signed "Givenchy, Paris, New York" on the clip of this beautiful earring. The gold-tone border sets off the pearl. 1970s. 1" round. $100.00 – 130.00. (Top) Signed "Monet" clip earrings. 1970s. 1¼" long. Gold-tone frame is etched in a 3-D pattern. The oval pink cabochon is slightly marbleized. $90.00 – 120.00.

(Left) Signed "Kenneth J. Lane." Weighty red and white polka dot panther with a gold-tone bow and collar of pavé rhinestones. Emerald eyes with gold-tone nose and ears. 1970s. $110.00 – 150.00. (Right) Gold-tone wings complement the silver-tone spine of this dragonfly with a gray bezel set glass head. 1970s. $75.00 – 105.00.

Birds of a feather flock together. Signed "©CADORO," 7½" of black boa feathers flow from the 2⅓" gold electroplate swan. The swan has four marquees and two sizes of clear stones glued in shallow cups. A flamboyant lady by the name of Carol will wear this swan with exuberance and grace. Price $90.00 – 130.00.

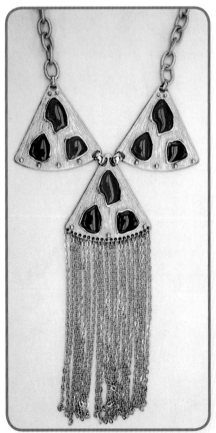

Stamped "TRIFARI©" at the bottom of the center gold-tone triangle. Measures 17". Twenty flexible chains are the highlight of this beauty. The gold-tone link chain measures 7¾". It attaches to three gold electroplated triangles. The cabochons are done in red and blue-green. 1970s. $110.00 – 140.00.

(Left) Original paper tag reads "VANESSA 054 Lot # 5704, $24.00." 1970s. Weighted. The two gold-tone chains with the single strand of pearls have a rich look. The necklace has four small royal blue beads. Measures 11½". $75.00 – 95.00. (Right) Stamped on the gold bar on the back "ACCESSOCRAFT N.Y.C." This is Penn State all the way — even complete in blue and white! The lion sort of resembles a door knocker. Measures 11¼", 1970s. Weighted. The electroplate gold chain measures 9¼". The drop is 2½" by 2½". $130.00 – 160.00.

The lion measures 5" wide and 4¾" long. The chain measures 9¾", the other with the fishhook clasp is 9½" long. Nice weight. Not signed. Matching clip earrings measure 3¼" long and 2" wide. Late 1970s to the early 1980s. The lions are nicely detailed. $130.00 – 170.00.

Stamped "INDIA" on the lower right bottom on the back. 6" wide. The butterfly is embossed in reds, blues, greens, and golds. Three gold-tone chains measure 7¼". Late 1970s. Butterflies are free to fly! $120.00 – 160.00.

This bold beauty measures 17½". Each side has five large open backed glass beads. Heavy enough to be paperweights. They attach to one glass cabochon that attaches to the 2" drop. 1970s. Unreal that this is unmarked. $195.00 – 250.00.

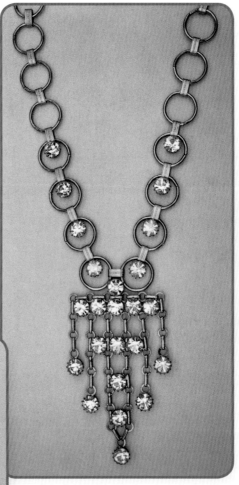

Unsigned. 1970s. Measures 23". Twelve gold-tone rings connect to four rings with stones. This piece is really fun and trendy and ever relevant for today's ladies! $170.00 – 230.00.

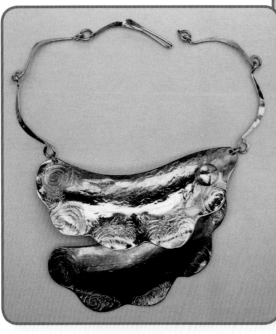

Signed "DESIGNED AND HANDMADE BY LILLO." The base is 5" wide with a 4" adjustable chain. This is done in gold tone and silver tone for the lady that likes both. A screw holds the two tone plates together. They are movable. 1970s. $150.00 – 200.00.

1970s. Signed "LES BERNARD." Three gold-tone chains attach to the drop. The drop has seven sets of chains with a spray of teeth-like dangles. Measures 11½". $155.00 – 200.00.

Big, 14½" long gold-tone links form a chain. 1970s. Unsigned. Reminds me of Mr. T from *The A-Team*. $120.00 – 150.00.

BIJOUX ELFE MADE IN ITALY. The round disc is stamped and attached to the chain. Measures 12¾". Gold tone and silver tone. This piece speaks for itself. $200.00 – 300.00.

Flower, 4¼" gold-tone pavé rhinestones. Three large petals are raised from the three small petals. The stem is 2¼" with a small leaf to the right. The center is done in pavé rhinestones. Looks like it should be signed KJL. It is unmarked. 1970s to the early 1980s. Weighted. Nice quality piece. $90.00 – 140.00.

Cleopatra coins clink! Measures 8". 1970s. Nine coins in four graduated sizes to the center coin 1¼" by 1¼". Each coins' front is embossed with "Napoleon Empereur." Unmarked. Weighted. $80.00 – 120.00.

(Top) This bulky 1½" double link chain measures 17". Late 1970s. Unsigned. $55.00 – 95.00. (Bottom) Late 1970s. Measures 15". Heavy gold-tone links. Unsigned. $50.00 – 90.00.

(Top Left) 1⅓" gold-tone hoops with a flexible dangling large faux pearl. Unsigned. Early 1980s. $40.00 – 70.00. (Bottom left) Monet, gold-tone hoop pierced earrings with a ¾" amethyst set in prongs on the top. 1970s. $50.00 – 90.00. (Right) 3½" neutral colored cabochons set in gold-tone open swirls designs. They are opened backed. Unsigned. 1970s to the early 1980s. They are flexible. $40.00 – 70.00.

15½" necklace, the first chain is 9", the second is 6". A large Lucite dark topaz ball with gold chains drops from the center. The earrings and bracelet match. Clip on earrings are both signed "BERGERE." $105.00 – 145.00.

(Left) This necklace matches a bracelet featured in another chapter. Four enameled sections are separated by a brown cabochon with the center of the necklace holding a matching cabochon. Unsigned. 1970s. $60.00 – 100.00. (Center) Late 1960s necklace measures 13". Unsigned. The center is enameled in black marquees with a frame that is star shaped. $70.00 – 100.00. (Right) Clasp on chain is marked "Korea." Measures 10½". 1970s. A Korean design on the gold side with the front side being done in a different design with silver and gold tones. Bezel set. $45.00 – 75.00.

Marked "West Germany." Weighty. Gold-tone choker with a 4" center that has a ½" black glass inset. $100.00 – 140.00.

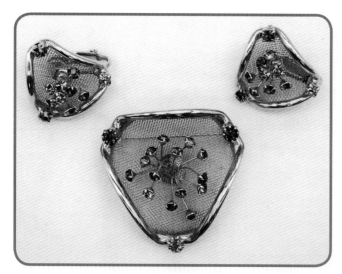

Demi parure set of a pin and clip earrings. 1960s. Light and airy. The pin is bordered in a gold-tone frame. The mid section looks like a screen, and there are tiny raised bars with small blue and green stones set in the tips. Matching earrings. Unsigned. $70.00 – 100.00.

(Top) 4" adjustable chain and a 2" chain with a fishhook clasp to close. The gold-tone drop width is 1¼". Each section is separated with a gold-tone bead. The two rows remind me of bowling pins. Weighted. Unmarked. 1970s. $75.00 – 105.00. (Bottom) 4" adjustable chain with the 1¼" fishhook clasp, the necklace measures 11¾". Gold-tone links connected on a chain. Flexible necklace from the 1970s. Unsigned. $70.00 – 100.00.

Leaf necklace and clip earrings. Gold-tone beads connect to the six leaf drop. It is done in browns, greens, and golds. Lighter in weight. Measures 10". 1980s. Earrings are 1½". Tricolored. Unmarked. $70.00 – 105.00.

Brushed gold, hinged collar with matching 1½" clip earrings. Early 1970s. Unsigned. $45.00 – 75.00.

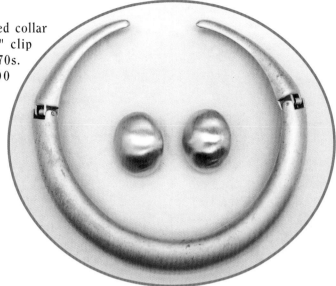

(Left) Unmarked. Measures 19¼". 8" gold chain connects to three gold-tone brown bugle beads that are separated by a round bead. The fall is 3" of gold-tone chain. 1980s. $40.00 – 60.00. (Right) 15" gold-tone chain with two faux jade cabochons on each side separated by a gold-tone bar. The drop is a pear-shaped faux jade drop that is tipped in a gold-tone cap. The diamond is signed "©Sarah Coventry" with a heavier outer chain that is a small three ring loop. The inside chain attaches by a small ring to the outer. It is a simple link chain. Truly one of a kind. 1970s. $60.00 – 100.00.

A swinging, retro-1970s discovery! This striking necklace was a gift from my mother-in-law. Ornately carved drops dangle from a remarkable pendant. Pendant is gold plating over metal. What a weighty piece! 12½" long; center 2¾" wide. Signed on the center and center of drop, "©Donall StannART." $200.00 – 250.00.

A ferocious find from the 1970s would make the perfect gift for any cat lover. This wild, large life-like lion pendant is suspended from a dazzling linked 9¾" chain. This little kitty is gold plated with a bone colored, molded plastic face. Signed "©RAZZA." $250.00 – 300.00.

What a splashy sunburst from the bold 1970s! This is my mother's absolute favorite summer sun. This Mr. Sun is blindingly big; the actual sunburst measures an astounding 5" in width and is upheld by a 15¾" chain. It's a weighty wear. Signed "KENNETH© Lane." $500.00 – 800.00.

Cleopatra, coming at you! This exotic psuedo-Egyptian necklace is equipped with nine squares accompanied by teardrops. In the center of the squares and drops are circular faux turquoise stones. Amazingly, this 1970s cultural catch is unsigned. The chain is 8" long and both the chain and appendages are gold plated. $120.00 – 160.00.

1970s era. She sells seashells by the seashore! Oh yes, this sandy find may be unsigned, but it resembles early Kenneth Lane. The 5" gold-plated chain is complete with five saucy seashells which are also gold plated. $110.00 – 150.00.

This gold-plated goodie could spice up many an outfit. The graduated Omega style chain possesses a blood red cabochon center with matching clip earrings. These classy clips are 1½" in length. Signed "Monet" on the clips of the earrings and clasp of the necklace. 1970s. $110.00 – 150.00.

(Top) A charismatic choker screams 1970s. Measures 14¾" when opened. Unsigned. Gold plated. $40.00 – 80.00. (Bottom) Another hot, 1970s pleasure that is 1½" wide. Two holed, adjustable, gold plated, chain bracelet. Unsigned. $30.00 – 60.00.

Fun for all! Lucky number 13. Thirteen bold, bouncy, beads hang in a pattern of faux pearl, gold, and gunmetal from the bulky 18½" chain. Fishhook clasp, so typical of the 1970s. Unsigned. $50.00 – 80.00.

This 1970s necklace makes many women want to play that funky music because it flatters any neckline. Gold plated. Very heavy and measures 1" in width. The gold tag is stamped with Ann Klein's logo and signature. $80.00 – 120.00.

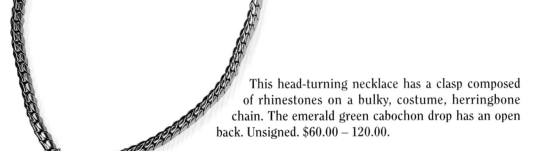

This head-turning necklace has a clasp composed of rhinestones on a bulky, costume, herringbone chain. The emerald green cabochon drop has an open back. Unsigned. $60.00 – 120.00.

Merry molded clear plastic beads, with faux pearls and a gold-tone cap enclosure. Measures 3½". 1970s. Unsigned. $60.00 – 120.00.

Looking for some haute stuff, baby tonight! This pin is certainly a class act with its double trouble mesh rings held together by small, solid gold plates. 2¼" of power pin! 1970s. Signed "Napier." $45.00 – 85.00.

A perfect slide necklace to spice up a white shirt and jeans. Suspended from the 19½" long rope are 1¼" tassels. On the back of the black side of the tag, it reads "Miriam Haskell." 1970s. $110.00 – 160.00.

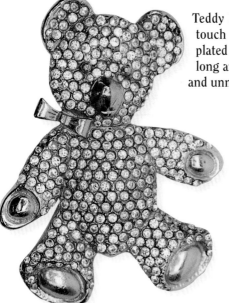

Teddy bear, teddy bear, turn around; teddy bear, teddy bear, touch the ground! Wow! This stunning teddy bear pin is gold plated with exquisitely detailed eyes, paws, nose, and ears. 3½" long and 2½" wide. Oh, that bow just finishes this cutie! Heavy and unmarked. Rhinestones are glued. 1970s. $70.00 – 100.00.

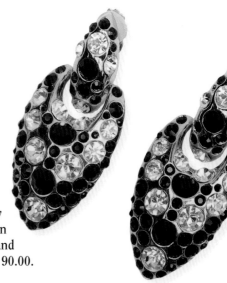

These magical clip-on earrings really hit the spot. Glued in rhinestones in black and crystal colors. 2¾" long and 1¼" wide. Unsigned. 1970s. $60.00 – 90.00.

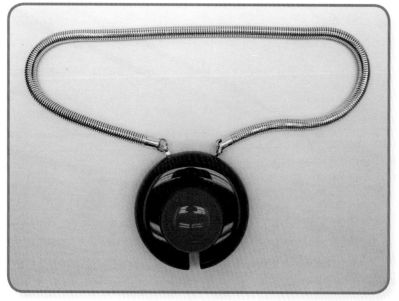

Lovely Lanvin France gold-plated rope chain necklace measures 8¾" and has a red-on-black centered drop. The cut out drop is 2¾". Late 1960s to the early 1970s. $140.00 – 200.00.

The black lacquered center of this gold-plated necklace is offset by its 10½" chain. Fishhook clasp. Early 1970s. Signed "©Monet" on the back of the center. $70.00 – 110.00.

A pin with punch! It is gold plated with 17 one-inch chains swinging from the detailed, half diamond shaped pin. Gold beads add nice detailing. 4¾" from top to bottom. Unsigned. Late 1960s to early 1970s. $60.00 – 110.00.

Charming choker/necklace is gold plated with seven clear rhinestones glued in shallow cups. Measures 17¼" long. Unsigned. Early 1970s. $45.00 – 85.00.

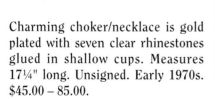

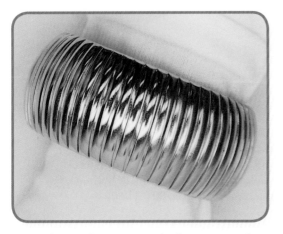

(Top) Great gold design resembling flowers is held together by seven links. Measures 6¾". Late 1950s to mid-1960s. Signed "©TRIFARI." $75.00 – 105.00. (Bottom) Another fence-like find! Electro plated with gold tone. Airy, light, and flexible! 7¼". Unmarked. Late 1950s. $55.00 – 65.00.

Expand your horizons with this nice quality, 1¼" wide gold-tone mid-1960s to the mid-1970s unsigned expansion bracelet. $60.00 – 90.00.

Creative cuff with deep engraving and a simple design. Gold-tone plating. 1¾" wide. Signed "Monet©" in center inside. Mid-1960s to the mid-1970s. $110.00 – 150.00.

Great detail. Should have been signed. Cuff bracelet with hinge. A rose on each side without the thorns. Mid-1960s to mid-1970s. $85.00 – 105.00.

Eight small seed pearls are set in the antique gold border. A blue, marbleized plastic center. Open backed. 2¼". Unmarked. Mid-1950s to the early 1960s. $65.00 – 95.00.

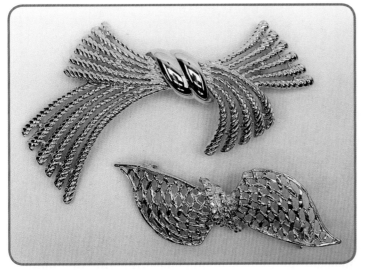

(Top) Heavy, gold-tone brooch with a rope design. Two solid rings are in the center. 3⅜". Late 1960s to the mid-1970s. Unmarked, unbelievable. $65.00 – 95.00. (Bottom) 2¼", unsigned pin. Open latticework is used on the ribbon design. Early 1960s to the mid-1970s. $45.00 – 65.00.

Happeningly heavy, gold wash over sterling. Stamped "NAPER STERLING." 1¾". Early 1960s. $80.00 – 130.00.

A knotted ribbon with a nice brushed design. 2½". Mid-1960s to the early 1970s. Signed "Coro." $65.00 – 85.00.

Demi-parure pin and clip earrings set with petals on each bend of the stamen of the flower. 1½" pin, earrings are ½". Each of the clip earrings and the flower are stamped "Trifari©." 1960s. $80.00 – 130.00.

Unique brooch with an open twig design with a border and center of raised, gold beads. 2¼". 1960s. Signed "©LISNER." $65.00 – 85.00.

A cool, lightening design with a center of pavé rhinestones. 1¾". Unmarked. 1960s. $60.00 – 80.00.

Peacefully pretty brooch with pearls glued in shallow basins. Double stemmed. 2¼". Signed "TRIFARI©." 1960s. $60.00 – 80.00.

Looks like fall! Gold wash over metal. Two leaves with a center vein and stems holding glued rhinestones. 2½". 1960s. Unsigned. $55.00 – 75.00.

Three glued-in aurora borealis stones with two black glass hearts in a pear-shaped cut hug the center vine design. 2¼". Late 1960s. $60.00 – 90.00.

(Top) The heaviest crossed bar pin. 3½". Unsigned. 1970s. $50.00 – 80.00.
(Bottom) 2¾" bar pin in antique gold wash over metal. 1970s. Unsigned. Weighty. $50.00 – 80.00.

(Top) Six prong-set rhinestones are in the center of this leaf. 1½". Early 1960s. Unsigned. $30.00 – 50.00. (Bottom) Pin is 2⅛". Signed "©Sarah Cov." Late 1960s. Leaf with a raised vein center. $45.00 – 75.00.

Art pin. The back is gold tone. Etched designs. 1¾". Stamped "Spain." Early to mid-1950s. $90.00 – 130.00.

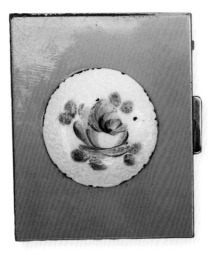

(Left) Pink enameling with a raised round design of a deep pink rose. 2⅛". Unsigned. Early to late 1950s. $25.00 – 45.00. (Right) Cute Coro pin. 2½". Mid-1950s to early 1960s. Gold-tone border with four small rhinestones at the edge of the cut outs. $40.00 – 70.00.

(Left) 1¼". Mid- to early 1970s. Signed, though too hard to read. $25.00 –55.00. (Right) Clip earrings on the original Monet holder. Clip stamped "Monet." Early to mid-1970s. 1⅜". $25.00 – 55.00.

(Top) Clip earrings with three open filigree panels. Topped off with a gold-tone clip. 1⅜". Signed "©Sarah Cov. Pat. Pend." Late 1960s to the early 1970s. $25.00 – 55.00. (Bottom) Coro clip earrings. 1⅛". $25.00 – 55.00.

(Left) Gold-tone bracelet. Does not open. 1970s. Unsigned. $20.00 – 40.00. (Center) Bracelet cuff with bezel setting. 1⅛". Green faux stone for the center. 1970s. Unsigned. $40.00 – 70.00. (Right) Hinged and safety-chained bracelet. Lightweight. Late 1960s. Signed "Coro." $40.00 – 80.00.

Heavy chain links with mother-of-pearl, wood, polished stone, and gold-tone charms. 7". Mid-1960s to the early 1970s. Gift from my mother-in-law. No value assigned.

(Left) Bracelet is gold toned with hinges. Design of engraved diamonds. Signed "KENNETH LANE." 1960s to the early 1970s. $105.00 – 135.00. (Center) "CORO PAT PEND" bracelet. Looks like Miami to me! Seashells, coral, and faux seed pearls. 1960s. $100.00 – 130.00. (Right) Hinged, gold-tone bracelet from the late 1960s. The design is a heavy knot in a twist. $100.00 – 130.00.

(Outer) Unsigned necklace measuring at the center 3½" with a 5¾" chain. Late 1940s to the 1950s. Four weighted gold leaves detailed with two copper petaled flowers with silver tipped leaves that all dangle from the vine. $105.00 – 125.00. (Center) Bow pin signed "Monet Sterling." Measures 2¼". 1940s. Done in copper and gold tones. $80.00 – 120.00.

Clip earrings and necklace done in gold tone. All oval rhinestones. This set is true royalty. Necklace center is 3¾" with a 5¼" chain and 2½" adjustable chain with a ball on the end. Earrings measure 1" with one being signed "TRIFARI." $130.00 – 180.00.

Demi-parure clip earrings and choker necklace is made of gold tone with pavé rhinestone. The original Viva tag holds the earrings. Set in lions with emerald eyes. Earrings are on the original Brody's of Indiana, Pennsylvania, tag. Priced at $15.00. Lion measures 2½". Unsigned. Early to mid-1970s. $175.00 – 225.00.

Cute choker necklace with rhinestones set in the gold circle surrounding the lion. The lion's face is very detailed. Two heavy gold chains are used to suspend it. Unsigned. Early to mid-1970s. $150.00 – 190.00.

1970s brooch measures 3¾". Made of metal with porcelain flowers with two marquis stones and a round crystal. In the feather of gold tone is a single strand of hand-set rhinestones with two dangling, flexible rows of fringe. A metal tribal mask is under the flowers. $130.00 – 180.00.

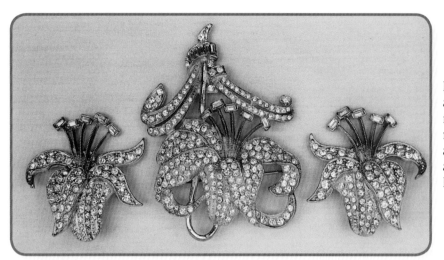

Dashing demi-parure brooch and clip earrings set. The pin measures 2¾" while the earrings are 1½". Both earrings are signed on the clip, "Astra," and on the lead "ORA." 1970s. For the set: $160.00 – 200.00.

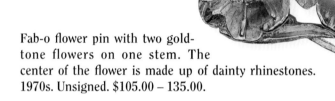

Fab-o flower pin with two gold-tone flowers on one stem. The center of the flower is made up of dainty rhinestones. 1970s. Unsigned. $105.00 – 135.00.

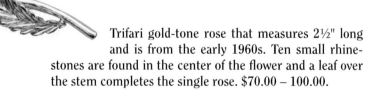

Trifari gold-tone rose that measures 2½" long and is from the early 1960s. Ten small rhinestones are found in the center of the flower and a leaf over the stem completes the single rose. $70.00 – 100.00.

(Left) 1¾" Trifari feminine flowing brooch from the 1960s is done in gold tone. $80.00 – 130.00. (Right) This Trifari gold-tone flower brooch from the late 1950s catches my eye. $60.00 – 80.00.

Majestic Monet rose pin measures 2¾". The clip earrings are ¾". All three pieces are signed. Quality from the 1970s. $110.00 – 130.00.

1970s rope circle pin with matching clip earrings, each with a faux pearl set on the inside. Each of the clip earrings is signed on the inside bottom of the clip, "pat pend." $85.00 – 115.00.

All three of these pieces are signed "Coro." The clip earrings and pin are in a raised jagged feather design. Earrings 1¼" and pin 3¾". 1950s to early 1960s. $105.00 – 125.00.

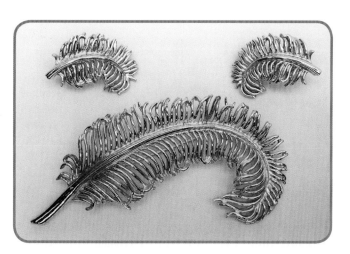

Six emerald-colored cabochons are set in brushed gold circles. Signed "DENICOLA." 6¾". 1950s. $140.00 – 170.00.

This 2½" gold-tone pin is from the 1970s. It has many amethyst, topaz, and ruby-colored, pear-shaped stones to make a lovely circle. $50.00 – 80.00.

Necklace and pierced earrings set. The original box was not photographed. Given to me by my mother-in-law. 25" long necklace. Signed "Jeanne" on the center of the necklace and each of the earrings. Rather flexible. $190.00 – 270.00.

4" Monet pin, original tag reads "Monet $15.00," and on the other side, "Monet Cassandra 1741." 1970s to the early 1980s. $85.00 – 115.00.

Lion on top of the pin. Decorative and ornamental. 3¼". Unsigned. 1970s to the early 1980s. $95.00 – 135.00.

(Left) Monet circle pin with black enameling and small rhinestones in gold tone. 1960s to the early 1970s. 1½". $70.00 – 105.00. (Right) This Sarah Coventry circle pin is from the 1960s. 1¼". $60.00 – 90.00.

Lovely Monet pin with five petals and open filigree work. 2¾". Late 1960s to the mid-1970s. $70.00 – 100.00.

Hinged, grooved diamond design. Weighted, cannot believe it isn't marked. 1970s. $75.00 – 105.00.

Elizabeth Taylor for AVON. Two gold-tone fish with cabochons, faux pearls, and small rhinestones. The drop is a flexible pear-shaped aquamarine. Nice quality. $115.00 – 135.00.

Stylish Silver

(Top left) Silver-tone wide cuff bracelet. It is an unusual design idea to have the bracelet hinged on the front where the design is. This is unmarked. 1970s. $30.00 – 50.00. (Top right) 1950s unsigned, hinged cuff bracelet. Winter scene is bordered by a silver-tone rope design. The bottom is signed "M. Wight." Four prongs hold the center, which is opened backed. $40.00 – 70.00. (Center) Unmarked silver-tone cuff bracelet with a center of faux turquoise in a bezel set that has a braided rope to border the stone. The sides are engraved with an Indian design. Early 1950s. $30.00 – 50.00. (Bottom) This silver-tone necklace in molded plastic is light to dark gray in color. The nine links are capped by a silver-tone bar that possesses glued-in rhinestones. The fishhook clasp is an adjustable chain that measures 3", the other is 6⅛". The back is linked by a staple-like link. 1950s. Unsigned. $30.00 – 50.00.

(Top) Expansion bracelet in silver tone with six ocean blue cabochons in a gold-tone cup; each stone is bezel set. Unsigned. Early 1950s. $45.00 – 65.00. (Center) Hinged bracelet signed "Sarah Coventry" on the clasp. Squares and rectangles in a series of six; each holds a faux stone. Fourteen links hold the closed back. Early 1950s. $50.00 – 90.00. (Bottom) Weighty, six link, silver-tone bracelet. The dark blue stones are bezel set and the aqua stones are set in dogs' teeth. Unmarked. Late 1940s. $55.00 – 85.00.

(Top) Every piece of this set is signed "Sarah Cov." The earrings are clip. The leafy silver-tone set is done with five petals that hold scattered leaves, which are set through out the colorful cabochons. The cabochons are opened backed. Six small seed pearls with a center faux pearl. Well crafted and weighty. Early 1950s. $85.00 – 125.00. (Bottom right) 2¾" round, open wire, silver-tone brooch with the center holding a small silver bead is signed "Sarah Cov." Early 1950s. $55.00 – 85.00. (Bottom left) This circle pin is signed "Sarah Cov." Measures 2¼". The stones are marquees and round; four different colors are scattered about the face of the brooch. 1970s. $55.00 – 85.00.

(Top left) Clip earrings done in silver tone with dark cabochon center. Signed "Monet." 1970s. $35.00 – 65.00. (Bottom left) 1½" unmarked silver-tone clip earrings. The center is ¼" raised molded black plastic. 1970s. $25.00 – 45.00. (Bottom right) 1970s. 1" unmarked square clip earrings with a center of molded plastic that has confetti in the colors of black and white. To the side, there are scrolls. $20.00 – 40.00. (Top right) Signed "Sarah Coventry" clip-on apple earrings. Brushed silver tone. $30.00 – 50.00.

(Top right and left) Matching clip earrings measure 4" of great black lead-type drops with silver beads topping the flexible dangling silver-tone spades. Unmarked. Late 1970s to the early 1980s. $40.00 – 80.00. (Center and bottom) Silver-tone bracelet measures 6". Six links of blue-green plastic are glued to the frame they are set in. Matching clip earrings. Late 1950s to the early 1960s. Unmarked. $45.00 – 65.00.

(Left) 2", unmarked, silver-tone circle pin is finished on the top right with two detailed leaves. The circle is raised. Late 1960s. (Center) 2¼" silver-tone sprigs in a circular pattern with the center of four sprigs. $45.00 – 75.00. (Right) This silver-tone bow is signed. 3-D; weighty. Late 1960s to early 1970s. $45.00 – 75.00.

(Left) This charm bracelet has six historical charms: 1884 Statue of Liberty, 1861 The Civil War, 1842 The Opening of the West, 1776 The Spirit of Independence, God created Heaven and Earth Stamped 1084, and a WWII that charm is stamped "STERLING." Clasp is stamped "STERLING." $85.00 – 105.00. (Top right) Looks like silver, this is not signed. Bird pin with colorful enameling. 1960s. $20.00 – 40.00. (Bottom right) Hand-crafted ring. Weighty. 1970s, each side is different. Large! $50.00 – 80.00.

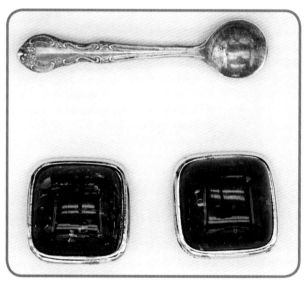

(Top) Looks like sterling, however is not marked. Spoon pin with nice details. Could have been an award from a direct sales company of silverware. 1960s. $35.00 – 55.00. (Bottom) 1" unmarked square clip earrings with a center of molded plastic that has confetti in the colors of mauve and red. $20.00 – 40.00.

This diamond shaped tag at the bottom left of the chain is signed "©Sarah Cov." Silver-tone base measures 4½" by 2½". The chain has a fishhook clasp that is 5", and the other measures 6¼". The 15 graduated filigree half-moons have nine silver-tone bars set in the moons. They are flexible. 1970s. $60.00 – 100.00.

(Left) 20" necklace done in silver tone with the drop measuring 3¾". The drop is weighted. Done in silver and salmon hoops and rings with a lone silver bead. A single silver bar for the center drop. 1970s to the early 1980s. Unmarked. $35.00 – 55.00. (Right) Original black and gold tag "T" with the crown "MADE IN USA," the other side reads "Jewels by TRIFARI." Measures 16½". Late 1960s to the early 1970s. The chain is comprised of orange plastic hoops that are connected to metal silver-tone hoops. The drop is a clear plastic triangle with a coral colored plastic encased inside. $50.00 – 80.00.

All from the 1960s. (Top) Measures 13½" open and 6¼" closed. Twelve faux turquoise cabochons set deep in a silver-tone flower of detailed filigree. Has matching earrings. $70.00 – 90.00. (Center) Silver-tone necklace. Unmarked. Fishhook clasp with adjustable chain. 1960s. $35.00 – 55.00. (Bottom) Silver-tone necklace with 11 leaves is unmarked. Adjustable chain with fishhook clasp. 1960s. $45.00 – 65.00.

Curiosity didn't kill this cat. Silver-tone cat. Late 1960s to the early 1970s. The cat has sparkling rhinestone eyes, which complement the long silvertone chain. $55.00 – 85.00.

My hubby's number one pick. This shining necklace, with matching clip-on earrings, measures 13". The earrings are 1¾". Very heavy, very high quality workmanship. The cabochon center of the necklace is 3" wide by 2". The centers of the earrings are ¾". 1970s. Unsigned. $170.00 – 220.00.

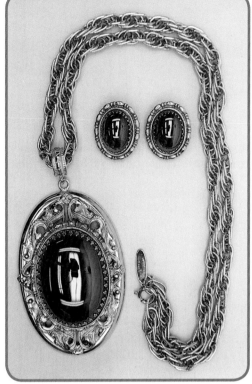

Flower power! This set is comprised of a silver-tone necklace and matching screw-back earrings. At the center of this bulky chain, you will find a five-pointed flower that has an aqua center. The center glass is held by four prongs. Necklace chain measures 8¼", and the earrings are 1¼" wide. 1960s to the early 1970s. Unsigned. $110.00 – 160.00.

Four bulky links connect the three silver-tone plates with a gold bead cap. There is a safety catch on the clasp. This charming 7¾" bracelet from the 1960s is signed "MARINO." $95.00 – 125.00.

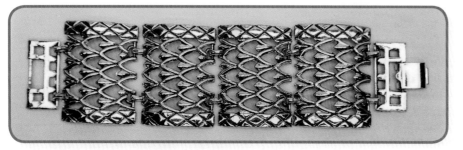

Hot and dazzling! This silver-tone over copper-tone stunner is 7½" of four large filigree links. Unsigned. Late 1950s to mid-1960s. $70.00 – 100.00.

(Top) Two rows of six chain links are set off by three ame-thyst, emerald-shaped colored glass and three purple frosted, emerald-shaped cabochons. 6½" long. Unsigned, I'm surprised. Late 1950s. Silver-tone plating. $80.00 – 110.00. (Bottom) Seven silver-tone links with round rhine-stones set in the middle. Six very small rhinestones at the ends. 7½" long. Early to mid-1960s. Unmarked. $80.00 – 110.00.

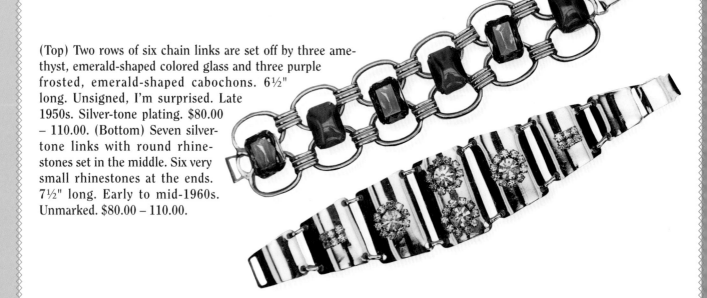

This very ornately detailed piece would make a perfect gift for a silver lover. The chunky links measure 2½" wide with applied detailing resembling a vine. Clasp has a safety catch. 6¾" long. Late 1950s. Signed "MARINO 5" on the tip and lock of clasp. $95.00 – 135.00.

Superb silver tone over copper bracelet. Very heavy. Six 2½" links are bedazzled with raised spirals and a large center ball. Measures 7¼". Unmarked. Late 1950s to mid-1960s. $70.00 – 100.00.

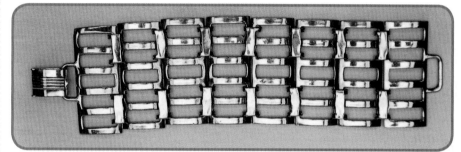

Fantastic fence-like bracelet from the late 1950s is unsigned. Eight 1¾" links total. Measures 6¼". Silver tone over metal. $65.00 – 85.00.

(Top) Sterling silver bracelet with six oval cabochons set one in each link. Nice detailing. 6¾". The clasp is stamped "Sterling 925 Tax Co." Also, stamped "Mexico" on the back. 1950s. $130.00 – 180.00. (Bottom) Six light coral molded plastic squares are linked together forming this beauty. Safety chain on the clasp. Measures 7". 1950s. Unsigned. $120.00 – 160.00.

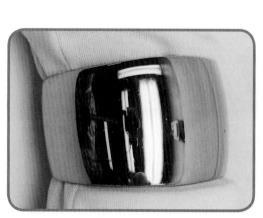

Simply stunning! This would be pretty with engraving also. This tiny silver tone over metal bracelet fits a small-boned wrist. Mid-1960s to mid-1970s. $60.00 – 80.00.

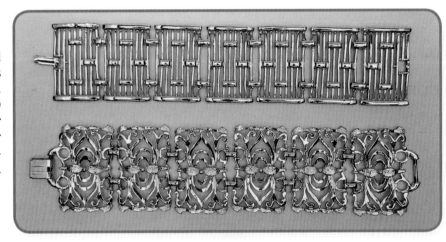

(Top) How pastoral a scene! This bracelet is made of gold over brass. Bezel set, hand painted on porcelain. Designs of birds, flowers, deer, and water. Safety chain on the clasp. 7¼". 1900 to the 1920s. Unsigned. $120.00 – 150.00. (Bottom) Gold tone over brass. ½" lava cameos. Design in high carving or relief. 6¾". Clasp is stamped "083." Late 1800s to the mid-1900s. $180.00 – 250.00.

(Top) Silver-tone plated bracelet with seven links held by two sets of two links. 7". 1950s. Unsigned. $95.00 – 125.00. (Bottom) Rather attractive gold tone over metal bracelet that is comprised of six links. 7¼". 1950s. $95.00 – 125.00.

(Top) This luminescent bracelet has multiple domes of Lucite with confetti sprinkles. 7" long, 1½" wide. Unsigned. 1950s. $110.00 – 190.00. (Bottom) This bracelet is made of silver tone over metal with white Lucite holding elegant pastel confetti. 6¾" long by 1½" wide. Signed "©PAM." 1950s. $110.00 – 140.00.

(Top) Fabulous flecks! These clip earrings have gold sparkles with black and white flecks encased in plastic. 1¼". Unsigned. 1950s. $45.00 – 65.00. (Bottom) Antique silver tone with insets of 2" black onyx. 7¾" long by 2" wide. 1950s. Unsigned. Nice bracelet. $130.00 – 170.00.

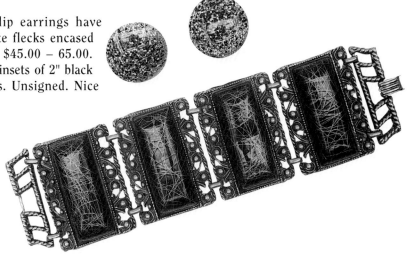

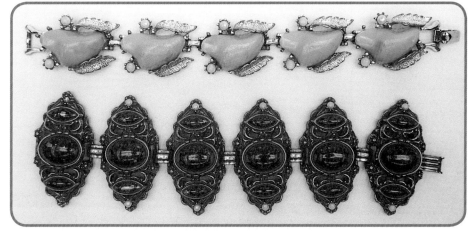

(Top) This silver-tone bracelet has leaves with faux seed pearls on each side of the faux turquoise stones. 7¼" long. 1950s. Signed "Coro." 1950s. $120.00 – 160.00. (Bottom) This bracelet has an antique silver-tone look with two royal blue cabochons in marquee settings. 2" wide by 6¾". 1950s. Unsigned. $105.00 – 125.00.

(Top) Daring, signed "STAR," designer bracelet. One link holds these eight, pink, wispy plastic links in silver tone, together. 1950s. 7". $115.00 – 145.00. (Bottom) Seven silver-tone bars with an engraved design on each side of the amethyst dome. Closed backing. 6¾" long. Unsigned. 1950s. $110.00 – 150.00.

I love this one! Reminds me of Waylon Jennings and Jessie Coulter. Silver tone for sweet singing songbirds. Six faux turquoise on each side of the three rows of beads. The center is the top for the base of the 2¼" wide drop. Measures 15". 1970s. Unsigned. $175.00 – 225.00.

Demi-parure. Rhodium plated. The brooch is 2¾" and the earrings are 1". Signed "TRIFARI 1960s." Four large sections with a jagged design. In the center is the star. $135.00 – 165.00.

Marvelous swirl design with a center faux pearl. Rhodium. Measures 2½". 1960s. Brooch is signed "SARAH COV." $130.00 – 150.00. Earrings measure 1½" and are of a similar design. Great center knot. 1960s. $55.00 – 75.00.

Demi-parure silver-tone clip earrings and brooch. Brooch measures 2½" and the earrings are 1⅜". All are unmarked. Flowers in 3-D with a center aurora borealis stone in each flower. Not 100% quality, yet attractive to the eye. Weighted. 1950s to the early 1960s. For the set, $105.00 – 135.00.

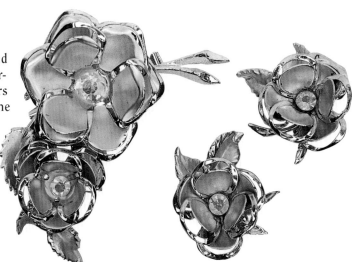

Signed "Sarah Cov" on each piece. Mid-1950s to the early 1960s. Brooch is 2⅜" with earrings measuring at 1¼". These remind me of free spirited people. For the set, $100.00 – 130.00.

(Top) Pin is weighted, unsigned, and measures 1¾". It is a design of graduated silver wire bars. Mid-1950s to the early 1960s. Attention getting. $90.00 – 120.00. (Bottom) Signed "STERLING" twice on each piece. Earrings are 1¼". Mid-1950s to the 1960s. $45.00 – 65.00.

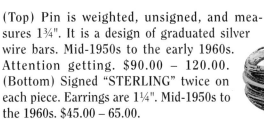

This flower brooch is 3¼". Unsigned. Jagged petals off of two rows of flowers. A center of silver-tone beads. 1950s. Unsigned. $65.00 – 105.00.

Signed "Lisner" on the clasp of the bracelet and the clips of the earrings. You are sure to look stunning in silver in this set. Late 1950s to the mid-1960s. Bracelet measures 7½" and the earrings are 1⅛". $120.00 – 160.00.

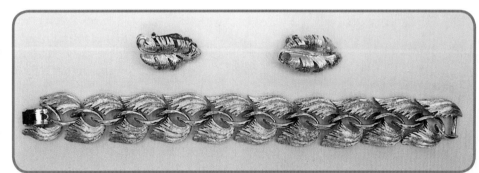

Bracelet is signed "Sarah Cov." Each of the clip earrings is signed "Sarah Cov." at the top and "pat pend Sarah Cov." on the bottom. Bracelet measures 7½", earrings measure ¾". Simple and statement making. You could dress this up or wear it very casually. Four links connect the five links of the bezel set black plastic. If you are a lover of silver and black, this set has your name on it. $125.00 – 155.00.

(From top to bottom) Silver-tone bracelet, unsigned. 1970s. Measures 7". Holds one charm. $30.00 – 50.00. Weighted 7" silver-tone bracelet unmarked from the 1970s. Two rows of chains with round flat ¾" silver plates. $55.00 – 85.00. Bulky chain bracelet 7¼" long. Silver tone, unmarked. 1950s. Mother Mary charm signed "1930 ITALY" with a cross and stars on the back of the charm. $80.00 – 120.00. 7¼" single chain silver-tone bracelet with one charm. Signed "A + Z STERLING" on the clasp. $50.00 – 80.00.

Signed "Coro" on the clasp of this necklace. Measures 5½". Late 1950s to the early 1960s. A great heart design held by a silver link. 4¼" adjustable chain with a fishhook clasp. $70.00 – 100.00.

The fishhook clasp of this choker measuring 5¾" is signed "Coro." The adjustable chain is 3¾". Early 1950s to the late 1960s. $85.00 – 105.00.

An unsolved mystery. Can you identify this woman? Pendant in silver tone that opens to hold a special photo on each side. I opened this and was surprised to find the original black and white picture of a lady on the right side. Unmarked. Early 1950s. This measures 1½". $100.00 – 130.00.

(Left) Unsigned pin measuring 1½". 1950s. Silver tone. Enclosed back. Round stone set in dog teeth. $60.00 – 80.00. (Right) Unsigned pin measuring 1½". Abalone is open back. Front abalone is held in place with six prongs. Enclosed in a swirl design. Late 1950s. $115.00 – 135.00.

(Top) Clip earrings, each signed "STERLING RS DENMARK." 1950s. Measures 1⅛". $45.00 – 75.00. (Bottom) Brooch that converts to a pendant. Early 1950s. Signed "STERLING AP TAZCC 325." Measures 1¾" in a triangle design with tiger's eye and an abalone owl. A star of abalone on the bottom right. $130.00 – 150.00.

This pin, signed "STERLING UL MEXICO 825," is sure to be a wow-er for spring break in Mexico! Measures 1½". One of the screw-back earrings has the same signature. Earrings each measure 1". Abalone and silver. 1950s. $130.00 – 160.00.

Bracelet measuring 7¼", signed "EM MEXICO TAM" on the clasp. Five links of silver-beaded squares holding 1⅛" of green molded plastic. 1950s. $110.00 – 150.00.

(Left) Cuff bracelet from the 1950s. Unsigned. Twisted rope design in silver. Weighty. $50.00 – 70.00. (Center) Signed "Sterling," from the 1950s. Raised center beads on the bracelet. Simple in style. Fits a very small wrist. $40.00 – 60.00. (Right) Cuff bracelet signed "PEWTER BDA," from the 1950s. $90.00 – 120.00.

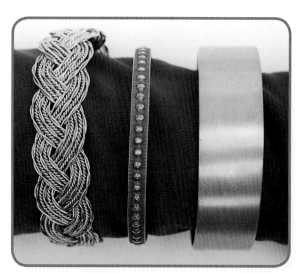

Pin is signed "SIAM STERLING" and measures 2½". Earrings measure 1¼". Each of the earrings is signed "SIAM STERLING." 1950s. As always, nice detailing on Siam Sterling. $125.00 – 155.00.

(Top, left) Clip earrings signed "STERLING CORO." 1940s. Two leaves with a rose. $55.00 – 95.00. (Top, right) Screw earrings. Metal flowers each with a center rhinestone. $40.00 – 50.00. (Rows 2 and 3) Seeing double! 7⅛" metal bracelets. Two leaves hold a flower with a center rhinestone. Done in six flowers linked by 12 metal ring links. $60.00 – 120.00. (Row 4, left) Sterling signed pin. 1¾". Three metal roses with a center rhinestone on a single vine with four leaves. $50.00 – 80.00. (Row 5, right) Four-rose circle pin measuring 1¾". Rose has a center rhinestone. Heavy. $50.00 – 80.00. (Bottom) Necklace, 6" of flowers, 9½" of chain. Five metal flowers are set on top of two leaves with a center rhinestone. $100.00 – 140.00.

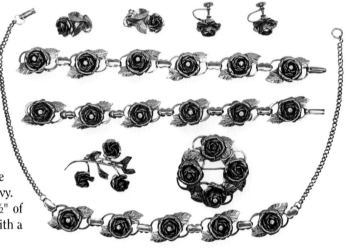

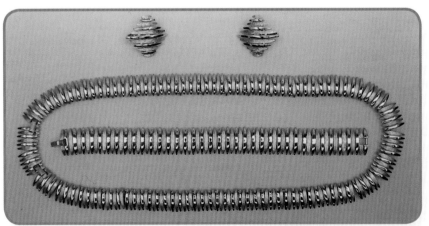

Matching clip earrings, bracelet, and necklace. The necklace is signed twice on each clasp. Each of the clip earrings is signed, and the clasp on the bracelet is signed "TRIFARI." 1950s. Silver tone in style of the 1950s. The necklace measures 10½" closed. Late 1950s. $115.00 – 145.00.

Signed Lisner necklace in silver tone. Done in a leaf pattern. Heavy 3¾" adjustable chain with a ball drop. Clip earrings signed "TRIFARI." Each one has a simple silver-tone leaf. 1950s. For the set: $50.00 – 80.00.

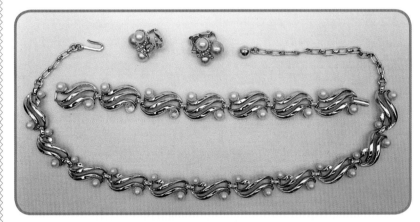

Clip earrings, signed "TRIFARI" with three pearls in a figure eight pattern of paste rhinestones from the 1950s. $50.00 – 80.00. Demi-parure bracelet signed "TRIFARI" on clasp with the necklace being signed on the fishhook clasp. The bracelet measures 7" and has two small pearls missing. The necklace measures 6" of adjustable chain with a silver ball to drop. Eleven links in two rows with a small pearl at each end held by a single silver link. 1950s. For the set: $105.00 – 145.00.

(Top) Lisner screw-on earrings in silver tone. From the 1950s. $40.00 – 60.00. (Bottom) Monet clip earrings. ¾". From the 1950s to the early 1960s. $40.00 – 60.00.

Coro, silver-tone pin from the 1950s. 1¾" of two rows of silver tone spun in a flower design with a raised center. $50.00 – 70.00.

(Top) STAR silver-tone screw-on earrings. 1960s. 1". $35.00 – 65.00. (Bottom) Sarah Coventry clip earrings. 1¼". 1960s. $40.00 – 60.00.

(Top) Trifari clip earrings. Silver-tone jagged edges with a tulip shape. 1960s. $35.00 – 65.00. (Bottom) Trifari clip earrings in silver tone from the 1960s. A leaf borders the silver beaded center. $35.00 – 65.00.

(Top) DANECRAFT STERLING screw-on earrings. ½". From the 1950s. $35.00 – 55.00. (Bottom) "FORSTNER STERLING" signed on the pin. The ¾" earrings are signed "STERLING." Two silver-tone rings with a dainty group of flowers make this a cutie. 1950. $95.00 – 135.00.

"Trifari" signed on each piece. Clip earrings ¾" and pin 2¾". 1960s, silver tone is functional. $85.00 – 125.00.

(Top) Beau Sterling four leaf clover pin with a center faux pearl set on sprigs of silver. 1950s. 2½". $60.00 – 90.00. (Bottom) 1½" filigree flower pin from the 1950s. Unsigned. $45.00 – 65.00.

Unsigned pin from the 1950s. Two sizes of three leaves are raised. Tips are sharp. Weighted. 2⅛". $65.00 – 95.00.

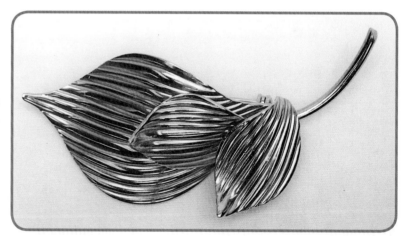

Flashy feather pin signed "Trifari" measures 3¼". 1960s. $70.00 – 110.00.

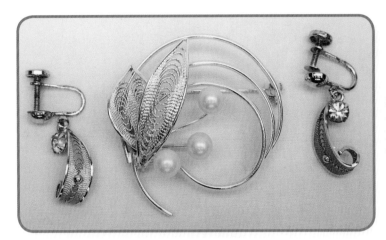

(Outer) Sterling screw-on earrings, 1" with a single prong-set rhinestone. 1960s. $35.00 – 55.00. (Inner) Delicate 1950s silver-tone pin is 1½" with three faux pearls set off of the open filigree leaves. $105.00 – 115.00.

Flower brooch is 3¼" with 1½" clip earrings. These bright starbursts have five petals, each with a center aurora borealis. Late 1950s to the mid-1960s. $105.00 – 125.00.

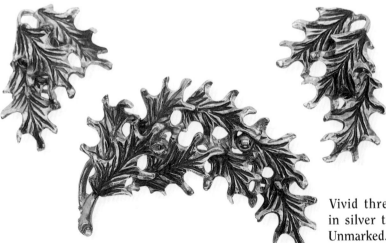

Vivid three leaf design for the 1960s. 2½" pin in silver tone. Matching clip earrings are 1¾". Unmarked. $90.00 – 120.00.

Bow-wow! Bow-wow! for the pretty poodle sweater pins. Complete with onyx eyes. 1950s. Unmarked. $55.00 – 85.00.

(Left) SANCREST M 1970s turquoise necklace. Measures 1¼" . $100.00 – 120.00. (Right) Unsigned cross. 2½" with a chain of 11½". 1970s. $115.00 – 145.00.

1950s. 2⅛" weighted leaf pin with a center silver ball with matching clip earrings. Nice workmanship for an unsigned set. $110.00 – 140.00.

Summertime Fun!

(Top) A heavy 1950s expansion bracelet. Signed "JAPAN." White glass beads with silver tips. Bracelet is silver tone. $50.00 – 70.00. (Center) 1950s plastic expansion bracelet strung on double sets of heavy string. $30.00 – 40.00. (Bottom) Plastic expansion bracelet strung on a heavy nylon string. 1950s. $30.00 – 40.00.

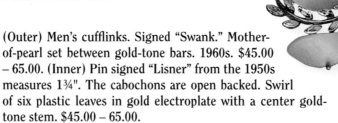

(Outer) Men's cufflinks. Signed "Swank." Mother-of-pearl set between gold-tone bars. 1960s. $45.00 – 65.00. (Inner) Pin signed "Lisner" from the 1950s measures 1¾". The cabochons are open backed. Swirl of six plastic leaves in gold electroplate with a center gold-tone stem. $45.00 – 65.00.

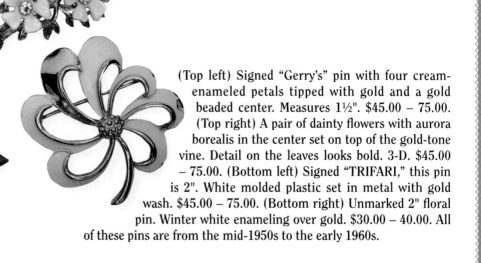

(Top left) Signed "Gerry's" pin with four cream-enameled petals tipped with gold and a gold beaded center. Measures 1½". $45.00 – 75.00. (Top right) A pair of dainty flowers with aurora borealis in the center set on top of the gold-tone vine. Detail on the leaves looks bold. 3-D. $45.00 – 75.00. (Bottom left) Signed "TRIFARI," this pin is 2". White molded plastic set in metal with gold wash. $45.00 – 75.00. (Bottom right) Unmarked 2" floral pin. Winter white enameling over gold. $30.00 – 40.00. All of these pins are from the mid-1950s to the early 1960s.

(Top left) Signed "TRIFARI" pin measures 2¾".
The back is brushed silver tone. Mid-1950s. $45.00
– 75.00. (Top right) 2¾" unsigned pin. The open
wispy leaf has white paint over a gold tone. Late
1950s to the early 1960s. $20.00 – 30.00. (Bottom)
Signed "Lisner" clip earrings from the mid-1950s.
A center of four rhinestones held between silver bars.
White enameled leaves on the outside. Measure 1⅛".
$40.00 – 70.00.

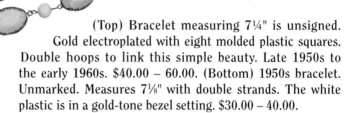

(Top) Bracelet measuring 7¼" is unsigned.
Gold electroplated with eight molded plastic squares.
Double hoops to link this simple beauty. Late 1950s to
the early 1960s. $40.00 – 60.00. (Bottom) 1950s bracelet.
Unmarked. Measures 7⅛" with double strands. The white
plastic is in a gold-tone bezel setting. $30.00 – 40.00.

Bracelet and clip earrings all signed "TRIFARI." White over gold tone, open lattice
work. The bracelet is 6¾" and the earrings are 1". Mid-1950s to the early 1960s.
$85.00 – 105.00.

Choker signed "CORO." 8½" center with 8½" of adjustable chain with a fishhook clasp. Caps done in gold tones show the 10 nice white molded plastic squares. Style! So 1960s. $75.00 – 100.00.

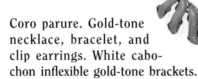

Coro parure. Gold-tone necklace, bracelet, and clip earrings. White cabochon inflexible gold-tone brackets. Weighted set. Mid-1950s to the early 1960s. Measurements are earrings 1¼", bracelet 7¼", and necklace 11¼", with a 5¼" adjustable chain with a fishhook clasp. Bracelet is signed "CORO" on the clasp. Each clip is signed "CORO" as well as the fishhook clasp on the necklace. A too hot to wear set, yet, this is one of my favorite sets for the heat of the summer! $155.00 – 185.00.

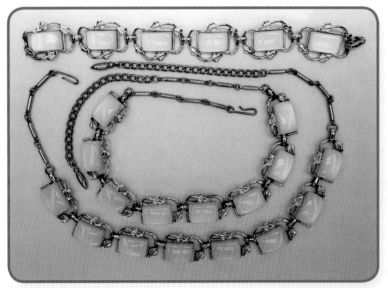

(Top) Bracelet is signed "CORO" on the clasp. Measures 7⅛". Six raised white plastic sets encompassed with an open gold-tone link design. Late 1950s. $40.00 – 70.00. (Bottom) You are not seeing double! This is a pair of chokers from the late 1950s. Looks like Coro, but they are unmarked. 8⅛" of chain and 9½" of adjustable chain. $50.00 – 80.00.

Matching clip earrings and bracelet, unmarked. Late 1950s. The bracelet measures 7¾" long and 2" wide. The earrings are 1¼" long. Winter white plastic with a gold-tone border. Closed backing. Striking! This set also would be great around the Christmas holiday season. $90.00 – 120.00.

(Top Left) Late 1950s clip earrings. Gold tone and multiple colors with four small aurora borealis set between leaves. One stone is missing. Signed "Lisner." $45.00 – 75.00. (Top right) Mid-1960s clip earrings. Coral color molded plastic sets in gold tone. Measure 1½". $30.00 – 40.00. (Center) Unmarked bracelet measuring 7¼". Three tones of molded plastic set in the gold-tone vines. Late 1950s. $45.00 – 75.00. (Bottom left) Signed "STAR" clip earrings. Two pea green maple leaves measure 1¼". Heavy. Late 1950s. $45.00 – 75.00. (Bottom right) Unmarked clip earrings. Late 1950s. Measure 1". Two buttercup oval cabochons in a horn of gold. $30.00 – 50.00.

Attractive Coro set! Bracelet has a safety chain and measures 6¾". The clasp is signed "CORO." Earrings are 1" with each clip being signed "CORO." The necklace is 7" at the center with 10½" of adjustable chain. Signed "CORO" on the fishhook clasp. Gold-tone open weave surrounds the butter-colored cabochon squares with a hint of pastel confetti. Mid-1950s to the early 1960s. $150.00 – 180.00.

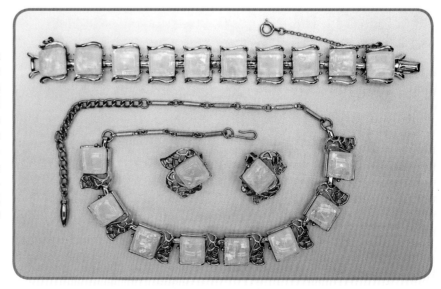

(Top) 7" bracelet done in silver over metal. Lilac colored molded plastic shells are open backed. The shells are topped off in lilac chaton rhinestones. Late 1950s. $40.00 – 60.00. (Bottom) Signed "Lisner" clip earrings. ¾" of a simple, yet stately design. In the center of the silver-tone circle is a cabochon amethyst. Mid-1960s. $45.00 – 75.00.

(Outer) Unsigned. Light purple marquee-shaped cabochons on a silver chain. The chain has a fishhook clasp with a silver ball. 6½" long. 1950s. $110.00 – 160.00. (Inner) Clip earrings. Gray, blue, and aqua marquee cabochons, open backed. Silver tone. Unsigned. Measures 1¼", from the late 1950s. $30.00 – 50.00.

(Top) Bracelet. Late 1950s. Measures 7" and has a safety chain. Ten links of silver tone with blue cabochons in two tones creating a flower with a center of aurora borealis glued in. Unsigned. $50.00 – 80.00. (Center) Ditto with the exception that this bracelet is pink. See top identification. (Bottom) 1" clip earrings from the late 1950s match the center bracelet. $60.00 – 80.00.

Coro, demi-parure. The chain of the necklace is 6¼" of adjustable chain with the center measuring 10". The drop is very stiff. All cabochons are closed backed. Bracelet is 7¼" with ten links of molded plastic. Signed on the safety chain. Colors of this set are greens and grays. Nicely detailed design of leaves with veins of three rhinestones on top of each leaf. Late 1950s. $130.00 – 150.00.

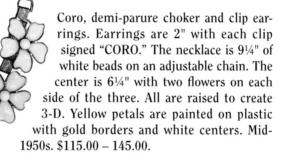

Coro, demi-parure choker and clip earrings. Earrings are 2" with each clip signed "CORO." The necklace is 9¼" of white beads on an adjustable chain. The center is 6¼" with two flowers on each side of the three. All are raised to create 3-D. Yellow petals are painted on plastic with gold borders and white centers. Mid-1950s. $115.00 – 145.00.

(Left) Pin. Faux ivory rose with a gold-tone stem. A leaf on each side. Mid-1960s to the early 1970s. Unmarked. 1¾". $40.00 – 60.00. (Right) Pin of faux ivory, signed "Lisner." Mid-1960s to the early 1970s. A single open leaf on the left of the rose. Measure 2¼". $50.00 – 70.00.

(Left) Signed "SARAH COV." Pin measures 1¾". Heavy braided rope in a double circle. Three gold-tone leaves hug the flower with a prong set jade. Complete with a stem with a faux pearl. Late 1960s to the mid-1970s. $75.00 – 105.00. (Right) Unmarked pin measures 1¾" with two faux ivory roses on a gold-tone stem. Enameled green plastic leaf on each side. Mid-1960s to the early 1970s. $40.00 – 60.00.

Necklace. 12¾". Hand strung on doubled string. The beads on each side of the necklace measure 5¼". Two sizes of leaves are in the center with a detailed vein. Sides have five leaves in overlay. Leaves in the center are separated by four beads. Heavy. 1970s. $105.00 – 135.00.

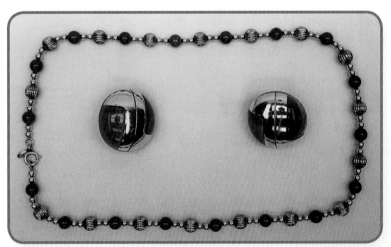

(Outer) Necklace. 8½". Marked on the clasp, "¹/₁₂ KGF." The tag is marked "¹/₁₂₀ 12KGFWRE." Two gold beads separate the jade, with a larger gold bead attached to the two small gold beads. Strung on wire. $110.00 – 150.00. (Inner) Clip earrings. Each clip is signed "LAVIN," 1970s. Weighted. Faux jade with two gold-tone pieces making one design in the center. $50.00 – 80.00.

(Left) 15" necklace. Fine chain link with ⅛" hand-painted faux jade barrels. Unmarked. 1970s. $55.00 – 85.00. (Right outer) Necklace. 8⅛" fine gold-tone chain with four filigree gold-tone bars connected by a bead. Three jade pieces are prong set and open backed. Signed "SORRENTO STERLING." $110.00 – 150.00. (Right inner) ¾" clip earrings, unmarked. Bezel set green center has a carved leaf and flower design. Weighted. Mid-1940s to 1950s. Great detailing. These definitely deserve a second look. $75.00 – 95.00.

"IRYA 2 WINARD ¹⁄₂₀
12kt gf." 1960s pin measures 2¼". Design
is a vibrant gold-tone whirlwind with three jadeite leaves.
$95.00 – 115.00.

This wondrous white enameled pin is stamped "Trifari"
on a gold bar. 1¾". Each of the clip earrings is signed.
The earrings each measure ¾". 1960s. $70.00 – 100.00.

Each piece is signed "Trifari." The pin measures 2¾" with the clip earrings measuring 1¼". White enameling over gold tone. The pin resembles the eagle. 1960s. $75.00 – 105.00.

These two beauties are such a fantastic reminder of summertime. (Left) BSK pineapple measures 2". 1960s. $50.00 – 80.00. (Right) Trifari white enameling over gold tone. This pin is almost tropical. 1960s. $50.00 – 80.00.

Necklace with tag stamped "Monet." 7¼" adjustable chain and 2¾" fishhook clasp. Late 1960s. $70.00 – 100.00. The necklace's matching clip earrings were not photographed. The earrings in the center are marked "Trifari" and are from the 1960s. $25.00 – 45.00.

(Top) Plastic clip butterflies with aurora borealis. 1950s. $30.00 – 50.00. (Bottom) Cute flowers signed "Made in West Germany." $35.00 – 55.00.

(Top left) 2" flag pin. 1960s to the 1970s. Rocking red, white, and blue rhinestones. $35.00 – 65.00. (Bottom center) Happy hoops. Red and white rhinestones in loops that are hooked together. 1960s. 1¾". $40.00 – 70.00. (Bottom right) Lisner red, white, and blue pin from the 1960s. Seven stones are missing. 2¼". $50.00 – 90.00.

In honor of the 1976 Bicentennial, both pieces are priceless. I know the owner wore both heavily. I am so proud of the United States military especially the United States Marine Corps! (Left) Spirit of '76 necklace. 2¼" with 11½" silver-tone chain. Signed "Cinerama Cranstan©, RI." Stamped on the bottom. 1970s. $35.00 – 65.00. (Right) Necklace. Reads, "Proclaim liberty throughout all the land." The back is nicely detailed. Pendant is 1¾" and the chain is 12½". 1970s. $35.00 – 65.00.

Banging butterfly pin. Yellow and black enameling over metal. 3⅛". Unsigned. 1960s. $45.00 – 85.00.

Mad about mothers! (Top) Mother pin made from plastic. (Bottom) Mother pin made from mother-of-pearl. The dangling star holds a small blue stone. The pin is marked "Skyline Drive." Each banner pin is from the 1950s and measures 1½" wide. $50.00 – 90.00 each.

All pins are unmarked, except the bottom left, which reads, "AUUA Made in Taiwan." Not your ordinary, garden variety array of butterflies. All from the 1960s, all enameling over metal. Prices range from $20.00 – 45.00. The bottom center bumblebee is enameling over silver-tone metal. 1960s. Unsigned. $25.00 – 35.00.

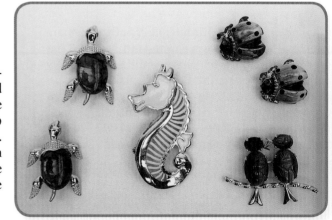

(Left) 1950s turtle scatter pins in gold tone with marbleized cabochons for backs. Measure 1¼" and are signed "Gerry's." $70.00 – 105.00. (Center) A 1950s seahorse signed "ORNK." Measures 2⅛". $80.00 – 110.00. (Top right) ½" unmarked ladybug scatter pins from the 1950s. These are my least favorite bugs. $40.00 – 70.00. (Bottom right) 1½" signed "BURT ⅟₂₀ 12K GF Cassell." From the 1960s. Two owls made of tiger's eye rest atop the gold-tone twig with gold-tone tails. $75.00 – 105.00.

Rhinestones, Rhinestones, Rhinestones

Bedazzling Bracelets

(Top) Perfect for the petite lady in your family. This topaz bracelet fits a small wrist. Measures 7⅛". Early 1950s. In the center of the three fringes is a flower design. All stones are hand set in prongs, and one stone is missing. The gold tone illuminates the topaz color quite brilliantly. Unmarked. $75.00 – 105.00. (Bottom) Four rhinestone flowers are done in pear and marquee shapes with a small chaton rhinestone in the flowers' centers. Three small silver links chain the flowers together. Unmarked. 1960s. Flexible. Truly one of a kind. $50.00 – 90.00.

(Top) This 1950s rhinestone bracelet measures 7". Gray marquees are set on each side of the hand-set chaton rhinestones. Each set of three stones have small aurora borealis stones set on each side of the rhinestone. Unsigned. The silver tone casts a diamond white color from the rhinestones. Unmarked. $80.00 – 120.00. (Bottom) Vision check! Seeing double! This aurora borealis bracelets are from the 1960s. The stones have a lot of fire. The blue tones show the silver tone setting nicely. Measure 7½". Unmarked. $55.00 – 95.00 each.

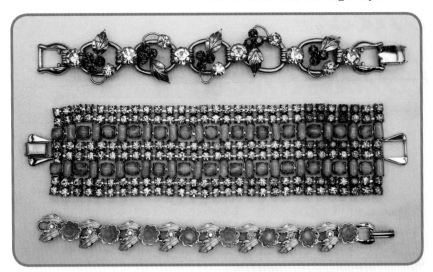

(Top) It's my "aquadisiac"! This bracelet measures 6¾". Five gold-tone links have a 3-D effect. The six larger aqua stones and the five smaller aqua stones are set in an every other pattern. The cluster of the three small sapphire colored stones is set with a gold tone leaf. Unmarked. Weighted. Nice quality. Early 1960s. $70.00 – 120.00. (Center) Six rows of aqua colored chaton cut rhinestones on silver tone complements the two rows of round and baguette handset cabochons. Unsigned. 1950s. Nice quality. 1¾" wide with 6½" of stones. $150.00 – 210.00. (Bottom) Signed "Judy Lee" from the early 1960s. The silver tone shows the light blue cabochon stones quite well. The eight aurora borealis stones are hard to see in the silver backing. As dainty as this appears, it is a heavy piece. Measures 6½". $65.00 – 95.00.

(Top) Antique gold frame with four faux jade stones. Measures 7¾". 1950s. Unsigned. $35.00 – 55.00. (Center) 6½" bracelet with four oval stones. Each stone is foiled on an open back. The chain link is a simple design. Unsigned. 1950s to the mid-1960s. $100.00 – 130.00. (Bottom) 7⅛". Antiqued gold-tone bracelet with multicolored cabochons and seed pearls set on each link. Unsigned. 1950s. $30.00 – 50.00.

Have a hankering for citrus fruits? This brightly colored lemon citrine bracelet should be signed as quality abounds. The marquees are large stones hand set in prongs. Twelve round stones border the bracelet which is done in gold tone. This has a safety chain. 1950s. 7¼". The back base has five oblong links to support the stones. $140.00 – 190.00.

(Left) Signed "Made in British Hong Kong." Expansion bracelet. Nice sized rhinestones. Weighty. $70.00 – 90.00. (Right) Expansion bracelet in a two-tone aqua marine. The emerald shaped stones are set in silver tone prongs. 1970s. Unmarked. $80.00 – 120.00.

(Left) Astonishing arms! 1940s bracelet with three rows of stones set in a slant pattern. (Right) 1940s expansion rhinestone bracelet. Three rows of rhinestones are set on silver tone. Both are unmarked and valued at $90.00 – 140.00.

(Top) Signed "Goldette NY©." Slide bracelet with a safety clasp. It is very heavy and measures 7¾". From the 1960s. $60.00 – 90.00. (Center) Rockin' rubies! 7" unmarked gold-tone bracelet with a pattern of rhinestone then ruby. They are set between the chains. 1970s. $55.00 – 85.00. (Bottom) 7" gold-tone bracelet set with a pattern of an emerald then rhinestone. 1970s. Unsigned. $55.00 – 85.00.

From left to right: Unmarked hinged weighty bracelet. On each side of the gold-tone beauty there are solid scroll bars. The bracelet design is raised scrolls. 1970s. $65.00 – 105.00. Looks like Whiting Davis, but is unsigned. The gold-tone bracelet clasps on the side, and the safety chain is missing. The top of the bracelet has seed pearls and turquoise cabochons. The center pearl is slightly larger than the others. $80.00 – 130.00. Bracelet is done with red and green enameling on brown. 1970s. Larger bracelet. Unsigned. $45.00 – 85.00. Multicolored cabochon slide bracelet from the 1950s. Unsigned. $40.00 – 60.00. Demi parure bracelet. The bracelet has five enameled sections separated by a gold-tone square with the centers holding a brown cabochon. 1970s set. (Matching necklace is seen in another picture.) Unsigned. $55.00 – 85.00.

From left to right: Mother of pearl, 1950s, circle bracelet. $55.00 – 85.00. Signed "Solid Brass 2o-Y-928-0010, Made in India." 1950s. Circle bracelet. $60.00 – 90.00. Signed "Made in India. Sangmv 1." Late 1960s. $20.00 – 40.00. Signed "India." 1970s circle bracelet. Painted green with gold diamond and sequins and small beads. $15.00 – 25.00. Unmarked goldtone hinged bracelet with a safety chain from the early 1970s. $20.00 – 30.00.

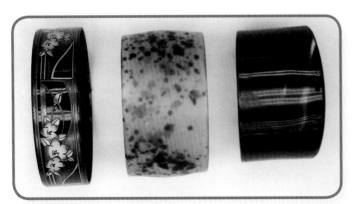

(Left) Signed "Michaela Frey." Metal enameled pink and white flowers with a black background. 1970s circle bracelet. Heavy. $20.00 – 40.00. (Center) Plastic 1960s cuff bracelet with brown and green confetti. $15.00 – 35.00. (Right) Cuff bracelet with brown tiger's eye from the 1960s. $15.00 – 25.00.

(Left) What happens in Mexico/stays in Mexico.... Silver-tone cuff bracelet from the 1960s that is signed "Alpaca Mexico." $35.00 – 55.00. (Center) Cuff bracelet in silver tone. Unsigned. The bezel set gray cabochon center greatly complements the silver-tone scrolls and rhinestone that it is in juxtaposition with. $20.00 – 40.00. (Right) Circle bracelet. Looks like sterling, but unsigned. Missing safety chain. 1960s. $15.00 – 25.00.

(Left) Hinged cuff bracelet in gold tone. With matching pierced earrings (far right). Citrine and peridot cabochons with small rhinestones are set in cups. 1970s. Weighty and unsigned. For the set: $40.00 – 60.00. (Center) How charming! 1970s, unsigned cuff bracelet. Gold tone with a pink enameled oval center that is set between enameled tear-drop shaped stones. $25.00 – 45.00.

(Top) Very versatile! 1960s unsigned slide bracelet. The slide is set between two chains of small faux seed pearls. $25.00 – 45.00. (Bottom) 1970s unmarked charm style bracelet. Charms are made of molded plastic in citrine colors of unique shapes. $35.00 – 55.00.

Perfectly pretty. Unmarked silver-tone bracelet with 10 blue molded plastic cabochons from the 1950s. 6½". $30.00 – 50.00.

(Top) An oldie, but goodie. Six silver-tone links make up this late 1950s unsigned 7" bracelet. $35.00 – 55.00. (Bottom) 1950s, dainty, rhinestone bracelet. 7" with a charming center design. $40.00 – 60.00.

(Top) Bracelet is gold tone. Two dashing strands of chaton-cut stones with three graduated stones on each side of the center stone. Measures 7" long. Unsigned. From the 1950s. $45.00 – 60.00. (Bottom) Gold-tone choker with eight aurora borealis flowers separated by nine aurora borealis stones. Center strand 6¾", other strand 5½", and the fishhook clasp strand 3". From the 1940s. Unsigned. $65.00 – 95.00.

Rhodium-plated bracelet. The clasp has a safety chain. Two strands of rhinestones with a center of nine emerald stones with three small chaton-cut rhinestones between. 7⅛". Looks like Kramer or Weiss. Mid-1940s to the early 1950s. $105.00 – 145.00.

A stunning silver bracelet which is quite weighty with dome-shaped, blue, cut glass. Two large rhinestones are between each, and the bracelet has a safety chain. Unsigned. 6". $125.00 – 155.00.

Brooches

Set your heart aflutter with gorgeous butterflies! Three butterfly pins from the 1980s. Gold tone frames the three blue stones that are set in shallow cups. The back is finished in a heavy gold metal. Each butterfly is unmarked. $40.00 – 70.00.

(Left) Sure to get any cat lover to do the stray cat strut. Whimsical 2" black cat pin from the 1980s. Center of the cat has pavé rhinestones bordered in gold. $30.00 – 40.00. (Right) Calling all dog lovers! This pin offers a new degree of canine fun. A rhinestone frame for "Duke." The nose and eyes are garnet stones in a prong setting. Measures 3¼". 1980s. Unsigned. $35.00 – 55.00.

(Left) Time to take to the links, golfers everywhere. 2¾" golf bag. This pin is enameled in yellow and black with pavé rhinestones. The clubs are topped with emerald, ruby, and sapphire colored stones glued in sets. Backing is done in heavy gold metal. 1980s, unmarked. $30.00 – 50.00. (Top right) Calling all Red Hat Ladies. This pin can be converted to a pendant. It is from the 1990s. Measures 1¾". $30.00 – 50.00. (Bottom right) Registered republicans, take heed: you too can don your support with an extravagant elephant like this. This elephant is fitting for Nancy Reagan. Measures 2¾". 1990s. Done in silver tone with pavé rhinestones on the body. A heavy silver backing. The eye is emerald green. Unsigned. $30.00 – 50.00.

Citrine marquees are prong set by hand. The 10 aurora borealis stones are set around the brooch with eight set at the tips of the marquee stone. The center round topaz stone is prong set. Measures 1¾". From the late 1940s and is unsigned. $55.00 – 95.00.

The peridots are in groups of two with a raised third to give depth. Three chaton stones in peridot with three aurora borealis chaton stones in the center make this color reflective. The center stone is a larger aurora borealis that is prong set. Measures 1½" and is from the 1940s to the 1950s. Unmarked. $50.00 – 90.00.

Lovely lemon shades! 1940s to the 1950s. This 2" pin is two-tone lemon citrine and topaz and made from marquee stones. They are hand set in prongs. The topaz marquees are smaller than the base and are raised to give this a 3-D look. The center stone is inset with a lemon citrine colored stone. Gold tone with a gold-tone backing. Unmarked. $65.00 – 105.00.

This 2" pin is prettier in person than the photo shows. Gold-tone sprigs hug the topaz chaton stones that are glued in shallow cups. Gold-tone backing. 1940s to the 1950s. Weighted and unsigned. $45.00 – 85.00.

Fall festival coming up? This pin is perfect for the occasion. This 2½" pin is unsigned. From the 1940s to the 1950s. Yellow enameling on gold-tone swirls around the lemon citrine colored stones that are set to look like a leaf. Unmarked. Brushed gold backing. $40.00 – 60.00.

Smokey marquee rhinestones in two sizes are set in silver tone. All stones are hand set. The center is a chaton stone. Silver-tone backing. This 1¾" pin is from the 1940s to 1950s. $45.00 – 75.00.

Uber-flexible! The pin can be converted to a pendant. The backs of the stones are open and framed in silver tone. Each larger confetti green marquee is set with a smaller lime green marquee between each stone. Raised centers of lime green marquees are set around the seven centers of olive green chaton stones. 1940s – 1950s. Unsigned. Measures 1¾". $45.00 – 95.00.

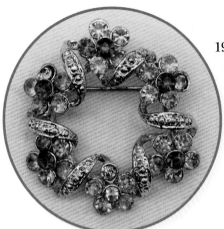

1950s delight! Pin measures 1½". Six sets of emerald stones are separated with a raised gold-tone ribbon. The stones are glued in shallow cups. This pin is a beauty. Unmarked. $40.00 – 70.00.

A gold tone sets off this emerald chaton pin. Each emerald stone is hand set in prongs. The border and center are emerald with the lighter green being set down in the pin, which makes for an optical illusion. Measures 1¾" and is unmarked. 1950s. $50.00 – 90.00.

A four leaf find for those who are looking to be lucky! Four leaf clover from the 1960s measuring 1½". The clover is bordered in gold tone with chaton pink, green, and red stones set in the frame. The green center stone is glued. Gold-tone backing. Unsigned. $40.00 -60.00.

This pin is from the late 1950s to the mid 1960s. Silver toning enhances the emeralds with crystal stones in a flashy fashion. All stones are hand set in the prongs. Light, airy, and fun. Measures 1½" and is unsigned. $40.00 – 70.00.

Signed "Sara Coventry." This pin did have clip earrings to match. Nicely sized center stone. The stone is bordered by silver-tone leaves with chaton rhinestones glued in cups. Measures 1¾". 1950s to the mid 1960s. $60.00 – 90.00.

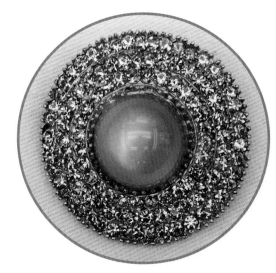

Pretty in pink! 1950s brooch measures 2"; it is unsigned. The center cabochon is open in the back. I like the gold tone with the pink it looks so rich. Chaton stones are glued in. $55.00 – 95.00.

This unmarked 1950s brooch is a fun shape. The amethyst stones are set in gold-tone dog teeth. The back is gold tone. Measures 1½". $45.00 – 95.00.

Bahama blue beauty explodes with color! This mid- to late 1940s pin measures 2" and is unsigned. The backing is gold tone. The stones are hand set in gold tone prongs. $50.00 – 100.00.

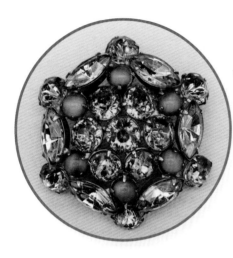

Weighted pin measures 2". This early 1950s pin has six chaton amethyst stones to border the six marquee-cut amethysts. Six small round cabochons are set around the seven round amethyst stones. All are hand set in a light gold-tone metal. $45.00 – 85.00.

1¾" triangle shaped pin from the 1950s is sparkling. The three corners are aurora borealis marquees raised off the amethyst marquee stones creating a nice depth. The center is made up of small chaton aurora borealis stones. Unmarked. All stones are hand set in the gold tone prongs. The backing is gold tone. $50.00 – 100.00.

A pallet of pastels is perfect for those who like the lighter looker of this starry eyed surprise. Pink, pearl, and purple stones make up this 1950s brooch. All stones are handset in gold-tone prongs. Notice the four sprigs of gold that are tipped with stars. Measures 2". $45.00 – 95.00.

Quality abounds in this 1950s unsigned brooch that measures 2¼" with a silver-tone backing. Each marquee is hand set in silver-tone prongs. The center of the leaf holds aurora borealis stones. The stem is silver with small black chaton stones. $50.00 – 100.00.

The Fourth of July would be a perfect holiday to wear this pin. 1950s, unsigned, and measures 2". Open backed marquees set in gold tone. Small aurora borealis chaton stones set about the pin. $50.00 – 100.00.

1940s rhinestone brooch measures 2¼". Marquee and round stones are set by hand in silver-tone prongs. Notice the raised silvertone bars with two sets of three glued-in rhinestones. Backing is silver. Unsigned. $50.00 – 100.00.

(Left) This early 1950s pin is dainty. Three-tone topaz stones in three sizes. Set in a gold-tone wire. $25.00 – 45.00. (Right) 1950s, pins are swirled together by a gold-tone band and a band of chaton topaz stones. $30.00 – 50.00.

(Left) Falling for you! 1960s pin in the shape of a leaf. Multicolored stones with a gold leaf top. The raised center rhinestone is prong set. $45.00 – 70.00. (Right) High quality fly pin from the 1960s with tri-colored stones that are foiled but open backed. $30.00 – 60.00.

2½", 1950s brooch done in two tones of green. Silver-tone back with prong-set stones, which are small. An emerald spine gives this a nice contrast. Unmarked. $40.00 – 80.00.

You've got me going around in circles! 1940s, gold over a metal. Six sets of five glued-in emerald stones make this circle pin. Unmarked. Measures 1½". $35.00 – 65.00.

Quality stones are used to complete the look of this piece. A 2" silver-tone brooch from the 1940s that has three rows of prongs that hold chaton cut rhinestones in a swirl design. The center is raised with four large aurora borealis stones, and six small stones hugging the fourth. Unmarked. $100.00 – 130.00.

A heavy hitter! 1940s, aurora borealis pin measures 1½". Silver-tone back. Weighted and unmarked. $65.00 – 95.00.

Unmarked and still stunning. The square shape defines this beauty. The fire in these aurora borealis stones is truly breathtaking. The gold-tone metal makes the fiery color. 1940s to the early 1950s. This brooch measures 1¾". Stones are all hand set. $90.00 – 130.00.

This aurora borealis pin has marquees and round chaton stones set in gold tone. Sets of three larger chaton stones are separated with a small stone raised off the three, which encompass the three marquees. Unsigned, from the late 1940s. $85.00 – 125.00.

From the late 1940s, measuring 1¾", unsigned. The bows are hand set in gold tone. The 3-D effect of the circles gives the pin flair. The larger stones that make the circle are set in a dog-tooth fashion. $75.00 – 105.00.

Measures 1¾" long, from the 1940s, and is unsigned. The top larger stone is foiled backed. Two sizes of chaton stones and two sizes of the marquee stones are employed in the piece. The stones are hand set. $75.00 – 105.00.

Thin wires make up the square border of this pin. Stones in wire are shaped to look like a star and frame the four inside stones. The aurora borealis stones are prong set. 1½", from the 1940s, and unmarked. Whimsical and not a great quality. $65.00 – 95.00.

Sleek and chic marquees and chaton stones set in a gold-tone metal grace the color of this aurora borealis pin. Unmarked, from the 1940s, and measures 2". Reflects more yellow than blue. $70.00 – 100.00.

True blues! 2", from the 1950s, set in silver tone. The wire is set in three with chaton and marquee stones set in prongs. Stones hold a lot of the blue color. Unsigned. $65.00 – 95.00.

1940s, white metal pin measures 3½". Each stone is open backed. Stones are glued in shallow cups. Unsigned. $35.00 – 45.00.

Signed "Coro." This pin measures 2¼". Two rows of chaton aurora borealis stones are glued in shallow cups. A center silver-tone ribbon of marcacite adds character to this pin. $70.00 – 105.00

This 1940s pin measures 2¾" and is unsigned. The gold-tone wash is worn on this pin. The two rows of stones are glued in shallow cups. Five stones are set in the metal sprigs. Unsigned. $50.00 – 70.00.

This 1950s pin measures 2¼". Topaz glass stones are opened backed. Gold-tone stars hold a small rhinestones in the five stars set between each stone. The center gold-tone flower petals are separated by small rhinestones with the center of the flower holding six small rhinestones. Nice weight. Unmarked. $100.00 – 140.00.

So glam! 1¾" two-tone yellow stones in three sizes make up this 1940s pin. Stones are glued in. Gold-tone metal tops off the pin with a drop that holds a dark stone that is foiled backed. Unsigned. $70.00 – 100.00.

(Left) Sparkling small 1½" pin from the 1940s. Unsigned. Gold tone shows the topaz chaton stones with great gusto. $50.00 – 70.00. (Right) 1" pin with pear and round topaz colored stones. Handset. 1940s, unsigned. $45.00 – 65.00.

(Left) Circle pin in gold tone with six blue marquee stones. Very delicate but pretty. Unsigned. 1950s. $45.00 – 65.00. (Center) Here, horsey, horsey! 1950s horseshoe shaped pin with faux pearls and sapphires. Light in weight. Unmarked. Whimsical! $40.00 – $60.00. (Right) 1950s gold-tone roped star with blue stones. The stones are raised off the pin to make this piece rather eyecatching. Unsigned. Chaton stones are hand set in prongs. $50.00 – 80.00.

(Top, left) 1½" silver-tone metal pin unmarked from the early 1950s. Could be worn during Christmas because it resembles a wreath with a bow on the top. Oval stones are glued in shallow cups. They are open backed with foil. Pretty. $55.00 – 85.00. (Top right) 1½" pin signed "West Germany." Delicate silver-tone filigree borders the pin. Two large, dark stones complement the four large, center aurora borealis stones. Four small aurora borealis stones top the darker stones. The center stone is missing. $60.00 – 90.00. (Bottom) 2". This early 1950s pin is unsigned. Rhodium to look like platinum. Pavé rhinestones with three aqua blue center stones. Rich looking. $65.00 – 95.00.

Terrifically topaz! 2¾" gold-tone brooch from the 1950s. Two shades of topaz with different shapes of stones are used. The back is open with foil. Unmarked. Weighted. $75.00 – 105.00.

2¾" gold-tone brooch from the 1950s. Emerald and sapphire colors are used. The back is open with foil. Unmarked. Weighted. $75.00 – 105.00.

Signed "Marvella." This brooch measures 1" in height. 2½" long. Done in 3-D. Silver-tone metal with all stones hand set in prongs. Three tones of blue rhinestones with turquoise cabochons and pearls. Center cabochon is 1". 1950s. High quality; well done. $125.00 – 175.00.

Original box reads "The Vatican Library Collection." The brooch is 2". Fiery colors complete the aurora borealis stones with smokey topaz chaton stones that are hand set in prongs. Gold tone adds sparkle to this brooch. $75.00 – 105.00.

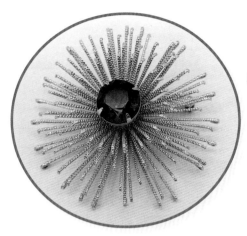

Signed "Sara Coventry." This had earrings to match. 1950s to the 1960s. The brooch is 2¼". $115.00 – 135.00.

Three aurora borealis rhinestones outline this pin. Eight light green, pear-shaped stones are set on gold tone, open backing. A nicely crafted piece! Late 1940s to the mid-1950s. 2" wide. Unsigned. $100.00 – 130.00.

August and November. These two colors absolutely glow together! Brooch measures 2¼". Chaton-cut citrines are set on a gold-tone backing and the peridot tapered baguettes highlight this piece. Late 1940s to the mid-1950s. Unsigned. $110.00 – 130.00.

Buzzing birds! Aqua and peridot marquee-shaped stones with royal blue rhinestones form a bird-like figure. A pear-shaped peridot stone is used for the head. 2¼" wide. Unsigned. 1940s to the mid-1950s. $100.00 – 130.00.

A gorgeous flower, indeed! Emerald and citrine-colored marquees create petals and leaves on this pretty flower. The stem is a delicate gold sprig. 3" long. Gold-tone plating. Early 1950s. $90.00 – 110.00.

Luscious leaves! This gold-tone pin has six large aurora borealis stones glued in to shallow cups; the other marquee-shaped leaves are made of small pavé rhinestones. Late 1940s to the early 1950s. Measures 2¾". Unmarked. $75.00 – 100.00.

Hot horseshoe! Frosty, light blue, marquee-shaped cabochons are set in a horseshoe-style pin. Dark blue small, round chaton cut stones rim the center. The marquee stones are open backed. Hand set on silver tone. 2" wide by 2¼" long. Unsigned. 1940s. $70.00 – 100.00.

Splendid sticks of light brown and aurora borealis chaton-cut stones make up this late 1940s Kramer pin. Prong set, gold-tone plating. $90.00 – 130.00.

Brilliantly bold brooch! This heavy-weight has five large ocean blue rhinestones with five royal blue round stones separating the larger ones. To finish the brooch, a filigree finish and sparkling center stones. All stones hand set, silver-tone plating. 1940s. 2¼" long. Unsigned. $90.00 – 120.00.

Banging banjo brooch! All stones are set on gold-tone plating by hand. The 3-D look completes the base of the banjo. Aurora borealis stones are used in place of the strings. 2½" long. Unsigned. Early to mid-1950s. $65.00 – 105.00.

(Left) Aloha, pineapple lovers! I love this pin! It can also be worn as a pendant. Gold-tone plating, 1¾" in length. Citrine-colored glass topped with a golden flower. The facets are highly detailed. Late 1950s to the early 1960s. Signed "Sarah Cov." $55.00 – 85.00. (Right) Fabulous flower-shaped pin. This is no brown-eyed Susan. Gold-tone plating, prong set. 1¾" wide and ¾" long. Unmarked, though it looks like Coro. Late 1940s to the early 1950s. $45.00 – 65.00.

Bountiful brooch of gold wash over metal with four faux pearls and eight pear-shaped faux marbleized turquoise cabochons and an oval center to finish. Converts to a pendant. Late 1950s to the 1960s. Signed "©Sarah Cov." $65.00 – 85.00.

Sleek and chic! Marquees entwine with chaton-cut, clear rhinestones. Measures 3". From the 1940s to the 1950s. Unsigned. Resembles a music clef. $70.00 – 90.00.

(Left) This beautiful pin converts to a pendant. Six blue flowers have blue rhinestone centers. Measures 1½". From the early Avon collection. $30.00 – 40.00. (Right) Five blue enameled flowers with enameled green leaves on gold tone. A dogtooth pronging holds the amethyst and aqua stones. Unsigned. Measures 2" long and is from the 1950s era. $35.00 – 55.00.

Vivid silver-tone bow brooch with a row of baguettes and round rhinestones. The baguettes are prong set and the round stones are glued. Measures 2½". 1950s. Signed "Sterling." $95.00 – 135.00.

Sophisticated circle burst brooch with three varied sizes of stones set in gold tone. 1¾" diameter. Unsigned. 1950s. $110.00 – 150.00.

This is a pin any jewelry lover would simply go gaga for! Measures 2½" in length. The glued rhinestones are in the shape of marquees, baguettes, and chaton cuts. Three-leaved beauty! 1950s. Signed "PELL." $120.00 – 160.00.

Hats off to this brooch! Measures 2¾" in length. Chaton-cut rhinestones are hand set with baguettes to finish. Unmarked. Late 1950s to the mid-1960s. $120.00 – 150.00.

A flowery brooch of marquees and hoops of chaton-cut rhinestones to complete the bouquet. 3-D. ¼" high and 2¾" long. 1950s. Unsigned. $120.00 – 150.00.

(Left) Chaton-cut rhinestones are glued in four rows with a center stone glued into a shallow cup. Because all the stones are of the same size, this makes the brooch rather striking. 1¾" diameter. 1940s to the 1950s. Unsigned. $110.00 – 130.00. (Right) Chaton, baguette, and emerald-cut rhinestone in a swirl design. The center is a single, lone rhinestone. Measures 1¾" and is ½" high. Unsigned. Late 1940s to the early 1950s. $120.00 – 150.00.

Great for a Pittsburgh Steelers fan! Luscious black and yellow rhinestones make this pin striking. The leaves have three rows per leaf of yellow rhinestones; the center stem is finished with black baguettes, topped off by a black marquee. Measures 2¾". Unmarked, I'm shocked. 1950s. $120.00 – 150.00.

Decorative brooch that converts to a pendant. Silver tone over metal plating. Marquees, diamonds, pears, and round rhinestones finish this hefty beauty. Marquee-cut stones are in clear and aurora borealis with gray-colored rhinestones. Loads of depth in this piece. Signed "Made in Austria." 1950s. $140.00 – 190.00.

Ornamental, three-dimensional brooch. Round gray stones, light gray marquees, brown oval stones, and a center brown marquee-cut stone complete this heavy brooch. 2" in diameter. Unmarked. Late 1940s to the early 1950s. $140.00 – 190.00.

This shocking gold-tone brooch converts to a pendant. All stones are set by hand. Oval stones abound in light gray and salmon shades. The center crystal is surrounded by 12 round, same shaded stones. Measures 2" by 2". Signed "Schreiner of New York." Late 1940s to the early 1950s. $150.00 – 200.00.

Super fly scatter pins composed of eight pear-shaped topazes. The topazes rise to the round center stone. Measures 1¼". Signed "Weiss Co." 1940s to the 1950s. For the pair: $90.00 – 140.00.

(Left) This gold-tone pin converts to a pendant. Two sizes of aurora borealis rhinestones with the larger stone encompassing two rows of smaller stones. Very fun! 2¼". Unsigned. Late 1940s to the mid-1950s. $110.00 – 150.00. (Right) Great detailing for this brooch. Larger stones are used to make it extra aesthetically pleasing. Marquees and pears on open backing; gray and clears on closed. Three aurora borealis stones scattered throughout unevenly. Late 1940s to the mid-1950s. 2¾". Unsigned. $130.00 – 180.00.

Brilliant butterfly brooch! It can fly into my house any day. The outline base is sterling with a raised body. Measures 2½" in the center. Signed "Sterling." 1940s. $120.00 – 170.00.

This smashing brooch is very weighty with its large, pear-shaped stones that have a small rhinestone between each. Three dimensional. 1¾" diameter. 1¼" depth. Should have been signed. 1940s to the 1950s. $115.00 – 155.00.

Wouldn't this be great on a black fur coat? The rhinestones burst is completed with wispy ends. The "wispies" are five tiny stones. Unsigned. 1940s. $125.00 – 175.00.

Quite charismatic! Green marquees hug the small aurora borealis stones in a gold-tone leaf. Topped by five small green stones, and the center is an aurora borealis. What a great gold stem! 3⅛". Unsigned. Late 1940s to the mid-1950s. $90.00 – 130.00.

Fantastic fly! This brooch has pavé rhinestones in shades of green and blue over gold tone and emerald enameling. Very heavy. 2½". 1970s. Unsigned. $100.00 – 140.00.

Brooch signed "Trifari" from the 1960s. Light aqua marquees and dark royal blue chaton rhinestones are glued in shallow cups. 2¼". 3-D in the shape of a half moon. A really bright piece. $100.00 – 130.00.

This magnificent butterfly brooch measures 3¼" long. Unmarked. Gold-plated wings with round peridots that are prong set by hand. The pear-shaped tail is open backed and nicely cut. Mid- to late 1950s. $125.00 – 155.00.

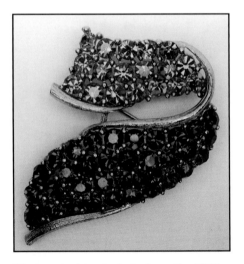

Unsigned whimsical pin from the 1950s. Done in the antique gold tone. Three rows of blue chatons on the top of the pin. The bottom row holds four rows of emerald chaton stones. The stones measure 1¾". $105.00 – 125.00.

This pin is unsigned. It measures 2⅛". Rays of blues and greens are really radiant. Done in a 3-D design. Silver tone with hand-set stones. This pin is nicely weighted. 1940s – 1950s. $100.00 – 120.00.

Pin signed "MADE IN AUSTRIA." Design is 3-D. Early 1950s. Dark and light colors contrast in the emeralds and peridots. Small silver-tone flowers are raised around the peridots and deep emerald marquees. A quality piece that is weighted. $105.00 – 125.00.

(Top) Scatter pins, unsigned, from the early 1950s. Each measures ¾". This square shape has filigree around the center emerald. The emerald is prong set by hand. This is such a quality piece it looks like an imposter of 14K gold with a real emerald! $80.00 – 120.00. (Bottom) Scatter pins signed "BARCLAY." 1⅛" of antiqued gold with emeralds, amethysts, and sapphire marquees separated by round amethysts with sapphire cabochon center prong set. Early 1950s. $90.00 – 130.00.

This unsigned brooch measures 2½". A bow done in 3-D guarantees to turn heads. The topaz and aqua chaton stones are set in shallow cups. Late 1940s to the mid-1950s. $115.00 – 145.00.

Looking like autumn to me! This 2½" antiqued gold pin is twisted rope in the shape of a leaf. Five leaves hold the fall colors of peridots and citrine stones in a scattered design. Signed "AVON." Has the look of a Florenza piece. 1970s – 1980s. $60.00 – 90.00.

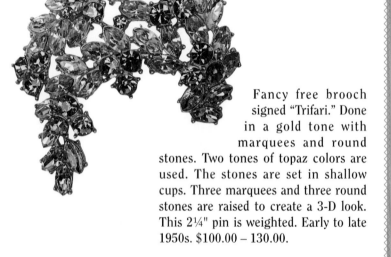

Fancy free brooch signed "Trifari." Done in a gold tone with marquees and round stones. Two tones of topaz colors are used. The stones are set in shallow cups. Three marquees and three round stones are raised to create a 3-D look. This 2¼" pin is weighted. Early to late 1950s. $100.00 – 130.00.

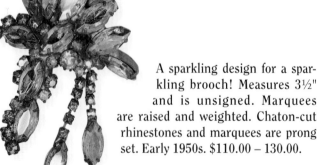

A charming flower brooch in a two-tone pink. Three small peridot rhinestones make up the stem. Stones are glued in shallow cups. Measures 2¾". Unmarked. Early 1950s. $75.00 – 105.00.

A sparkling design for a sparkling brooch! Measures 3½" and is unsigned. Marquees are raised and weighted. Chaton-cut rhinestones and marquees are prong set. Early 1950s. $110.00 – 130.00.

An exquisite aurora borealis rhinestone pin from the 1940s! Prong-set aurora borealis rhinestones make up the base with the aurora beads set up off of the base. Two rows of aurora borealis rhinestones with a large aurora borealis stone in the center to create a floral design. Measures 1½" and is unmarked. $85.00 – 115.00.

This silver-tone brooch is a delicate spray of rhinestones in marquee and round shapes. All prong set. Measures 3". Unmarked. Mid-1940s to early 1950s. $105.00 – 135.00.

Superb square designed brooch in a 3-D effect. Chaton and emerald shapes complete the square. A center emerald stone. The placement of the pin on the back tells me it is to be worn in the shape of a diamond. Done in silver tone which makes the pin look heavy, and it is. 1940s. Measures 1¾" and is unsigned. $100.00 – 140.00.

Heavy brooch, signed "Coro," measures 2½". Flashing to the eye are aurora borealis and molded plastic in rainbow colors. A silver-tone stem holds a set of small leaves at the top and bottom. Open backed. 1950s. $85.00 – 115.00.

Unsigned 2" pin. All stones are open in the back. Amethyst oval, round, and pear-shaped glass of nice sizes make up this delight. The center bursts with six small bars topped with small rhinestones. Four small rhinestones are missing. Gold tone over metal. 1940s. $115.00 – 135.00.

Sizzling 2¾" brooch from the 1940s. Silver tone with stones prong set by hand. Two rows of chaton rhinestones around the six light amethyst marquees. Two small and two large round rhinestones scattered. The light amethyst stones are open backed. Unmarked. $115.00 – 135.00.

This brooch is done in a gold wash over metal. Prong-set amethyst stones are open backed. Eight amethyst ovals surround the center gold flower with the rhinestones glued in shallow cups. Heavy design of three filigree flowers in a gold-tone circle with one small stem from the vine. Measures 2¾" and is unsigned. Late 1930s to mid-1940s. $120.00 – 160.00.

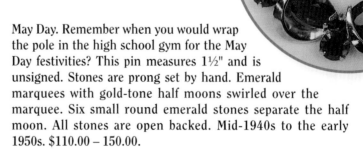

May Day. Remember when you would wrap the pole in the high school gym for the May Day festivities? This pin measures 1½" and is unsigned. Stones are prong set by hand. Emerald marquees with gold-tone half moons swirled over the marquee. Six small round emerald stones separate the half moon. All stones are open backed. Mid-1940s to the early 1950s. $110.00 – 150.00.

This fun pin is from the 1940s. It is gold backed and measures 1½". Unmarked. The beads are hand painted in reds and golds. Four are done in aurora borealis. The center holds a cranberry colored, oddly shaped plastic bead, with a center rhinestone. Each bead is tipped with a small prong set rhinestone. $80.00 – 110.00.

Both of these beauties are so Victorian! (Left) 1940s antique silver-tone pin measuring 1½" wide. Great open filigree done in 3-D. Peridot and emerald-colored stones are prong set by hand. Unsigned. Nicely faceted large stones used. $125.00 – 155.00. (Right) 1¼" antique silver-tone pin done in open filigree. 3-D effect. Light aqua and royal blue stones prong set by hand. Unsigned. 1940s. $125.00 – 155.00.

Appealing 1940s pin, unsigned. Stones are prong set by hand. Three pear-shaped dark topaz stones with two sizes of round rhinestones. This picture is deceiving, the pin only measures 1½". $95.00 – 135.00.

Brilliant designed pin measures 1¾", from the 1940s. The three-fold citrine colors are prong set by hand. Pin done in 3-D. Design of a circle in a square with citrine chaton stones as the circle. Two marquees make the square and four topaz chaton stones circle the brown center stone. Unsigned. $105.00 – 135.00.

Bold and bossy brooch measures 4¼" by 2½". 1940s, not signed. Gold wash over metal. Large citrine square glass held by four prongs. Eight petals on this flower with a single stem wrapped with the leaf. $160.00 – 200.00.

Functional brooch of the 1940s. Measures 2¼". Unsigned. Hand-set stones. Pink cabochon marquees with three oval dark pink and white finished with four small aurora borealis rhinestones are reminiscent of Victorian parasols. $105.00 – 125.00.

Splendid flowing design makes up this unsigned brooch. Measures 2¾" and is from the 1940s. Stones are hand set. Arranged in small and large sizes of light and dark blue marquees with small aurora borealis. Closed backing done in silver tone. $100.00 – 130.00.

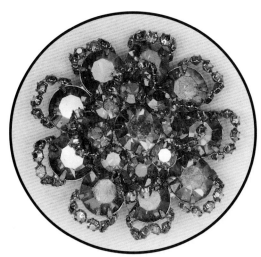

To wear this brooch you must be flashy. Done in 3-D effect with aurora borealis stones, and is heavy. Measures 2¼". 1940s. $115.00 – 135.00.

Attractive brooch is signed "Austria." Astounding workmanship in this piece. Five flowers of teardrops with dark aqua round stones embrace the center flower consisting of dark aqua round stones. Stones are hand set and done in silver tone. Measures 2⅛", 1950s. $105.00 – 145.00.

Pendant converts to a brooch. The magnificent Florenza from the mid-1920s to the early 1930s measures 2¼" with the purple glass measuring 1⅛". The center stone is foiled on the back. Aurora borealis and amethysts are set around the center stone on the silver edges. $180.00 – 280.00.

This elegant brooch is unmarked. Open filigree work separated by solid gold-tone bars. The bezel emerald stone is open backed. Gold tone brushed over metal. Measures 2¼". The stone is 1¼". Mid-1920s to the early 1930s. $170.00 – 270.00.

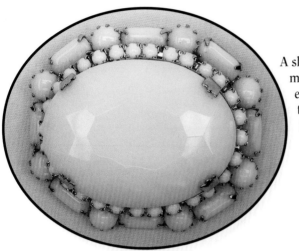

A sleek brooch with the oval center in white milk glass that is open backed. Round and emerald cabochons all set by hand. Gold tone. Measures 2" and is unsigned. Early 1930s to mid-1940s. $170.00 – 230.00.

Signed "KARU ANKE INC.," brooch measures 2". Antique gold wash over metal. The red aurora borealis stones are hand set in shallow cups. The decorative frame looks like a design of six jagged pine branches. Early 1940s to the early 1950s. $130.00 – 160.00.

Primitive, yet appealing brooch from the 1940s is weighted. Nice sized, well cut purple stones, two large and three medium, are glued in the sets. Rhinestones are sprinkled about. Unmarked and measures 2". Gold tone. $120.00 – 160.00.

Kramer sterling brooch is mystical in design. Round and oval rhinestones set around a raised center of nine chaton rhinestones with the oval center. Three silver wires flow off the side of the center, each tipped with a rhinestone. All stones prong set by hand. 1940s to the early 1950s. Measures 3". $140.00 – 180.00.

Weiss brooch measures 2½". 1940s to the early 1950s. Weighted and done in 3-D, the silver tone is fantastic in quality. The base is marquees with raised round rhinestones in a floral design. Three rhodium swirls of pavé stones are placed between two round rhinestones. $150.00 – 190.00.

Sarah Coventry pin from the 1950s measures 2½". This is a light, simple design of five aqua marquees that are glued in the shallow cups. Each is set between a silver leaf-like enclosure. Baguettes are down the center spine with small rhinestones around the leaves. $85.00 – 115.00.

This 3½" lizard is flexible from the arms down. Dark peridot and green-blue rhinestones are used for the body of the lizard. The spine is made of turquoise colored glass. A brown stone for the head. Silver tone. Mid- to late 1950s. Unsigned. $105.00 – 135.00.

Fresh from the dealership... This 1950s car pin is definitely uptown. The chaton-cut rhinestones are in the shape of a car with black stones used as the tires, window, wheel, and light. All stones are set by hand, and the pin is done in silver tone. Measures 2¼" and is unmarked. $105.00 – 135.00.

Sophistication speaks with this rhodium brooch. I can't believe this is unmarked. Heavy pavé rhinestones make the 3-D flower. Measures 2¾". From the late 1940s. $125.00 – 175.00.

Taxi, taxi, please, taxi! This 1950s cab reminds me of the old cabs in Pittsburgh. Topaz, black, and crystal rhinestones make up this car. Silver tone. Stones set by hand. Measures 2¾". Unmarked. $110.00 – 140.00.

This sparkling bow should be worn for the holidays. Measures 2½" and is unsigned. Chaton rhinestones make up the flexible ribbon. Baguettes are in the center of the ribbon. Quality stones. Late 1940s to the early 1950s. $125.00 – 175.00.

Butterflies are free to fly, fly away. Heavy Weiss butterfly brooch from the late 1940s to the early 1950s. Four sections of white glass for wings and a body of large and small marquee cabochons. Small red stones for the accents. One stone is missing on the top right. 2¼" wide. $90.00 – 130.00.

Austrian brooch measures 3¾". Elaborate style offers small chaton pink rhinestones with a single pear-shaped stone at the bottom right of the pin. Early 1950s. $120.00 – 170.00.

This 1950s hand-set brooch is sleek in the best way. Topaz marquees then aurora borealis stones embrace the four large round topaz stones. 3-D effect. $115.00 – 135.00.

Attention getter. Weighted, 2½". 1950s brooch. Pear, marquee, and round stones in a two-tone topaz color with six small aurora borealis stones in a circle setting. A large aurora borealis center. $100.00 – 120.00.

Circle pin with three marquees in the center. 1950s to the early 1960s. $40.00 – 60.00.

Unmarked 2¼" cross in antique gold. Four oval amethysts and round center with faux turquoise stones on the sides of the stones. 1970s. $90.00 – 130.00.

Saucy silver-tone plated brooch with larger sized pear and round cabochons set around the pink chaton cut rhinestones with a round center. Mid-1940s to the late 1950s. 2¼". $115.00 – 135.00.

Two bedazzling shades of amethysts are chaton cut for this typically whimsical 1940s flower. Unsigned. $85.00 – 105.00.

1940s bold brooch in silver tone with round marquee and emerald rhinestones in 3-D. Weighted and unsigned. Measures 2¼". $125.00 – 165.00.

A flexible pink pin with a tassel suspended from the bottom. 1960s. 3½". Signed "Sara Cov." $75.00 – 105.00.

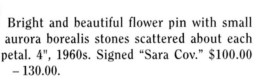

Bright and beautiful flower pin with small aurora borealis stones scattered about each petal. 4", 1960s. Signed "Sara Cov." $100.00 – 130.00.

Elegant Earrings

Flipping for flowers! 1¾" clip-on earrings. Ten gold-tone flowers set with center faux pearls bordering the center bud with an emerald stone set in the bud. Early 1960s. $75.00 – 95.00.

Just call me Cleopatra, everybody, because my earrings make me Queen of the Nile! These clip earrings are 3" long. They are from the 1960s. Ten strands of dangling faux pearls are bound by gold-tone links. The top of the earrings is made of green plastic with an Egyptian-looking face. $75.00 – 95.00.

Flora explodes from a fabulous rhinestone base. 3" long clip earrings really dangle and swing! The stones are opened back and closed back. The choice of size of the earrings and stones used are bold and beautiful. 1960s, unsigned. $100.00 – 125.00.

(Top) Unsigned clip earrings from the 1940s. The cabochons are nice sized marquees set with accents of aurora borealis. All stones are set by hand. Gold tone. $70.00 – 100.00. (Bottom) 1½" unsigned clip earrings. Frosted pink rhinestones in a marquee shape are graced with aurora borealis stones to add brilliance in color. 1940s. $70.00 – 100.00.

(Top) 1¼" of plastic base holds the gold-tone wire with light aqua stones. 1950s. Unsigned. $55.00 – 75.00. (Bottom) 1" unmarked clip earring. 1950s. The plastic base has small stones in multiple colors set in a gold-tone star. The stones are hand set in prongs. $55.00 – 75.00.

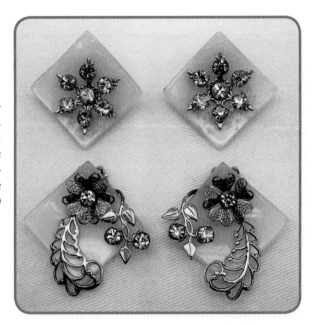

(Top) These earrings can be painful to wear after long periods of time. However, they are ultra-glamorous! Copper floral center makes the two-tone topaz stones shine! Measures 1", unsigned. 1950s. $60.00 – 80.00. (Bottom) 1" unsigned clip earrings from the 1950s. Three lighter colors of topaz in a pear shape with a round center stone. $60.00 – 80.00.

(Top) 1½" unsigned clip earring from the 1950s. The base is comprised of crystal colored rhinestones with aurora borealis stones in two groups of three raised to give this depth. Stones are hand set. $65.00 – 85.00. (Bottom) 1¼" unsigned aurora borealis clip earrings. 1950s. Two sizes of round stones are tipped with small marquee stones. $45.00 – 65.00.

(Top, left) "DOWN Weiss" signed on each clip. Six small chaton stones are set between each white baguette stone. All stones hand set in silver-tone prongs. 1950s. $60.00 – 100.00. (Top, right) Multicolored shapes and stones on black plastic. 1940s, ¾". $40.00 – 60.00. (Bottom, left) 1950s unsigned clip earrings. Three small citrine chaton stones top, center, and bottom of the earrings enhance the frosted yellow baguettes. $45.00 – 65.00. (Bottom, right) Looks like Weiss, but unmarked. Four chaton stones and eight baguettes border the emerald-shaped center. 1950s. $30.00 – 40.00.

3¾" of rhinestones in flexible loops set in silver-tone prongs. All stones are hand set. Three emerald oval cabochons are in a bezel setting. They are opened backed. Unsigned. 1970s. $125.00 – 165.00.

(Top) Clip-on earrings from the 1950s. Unmarked and weighty. Set in gold tone. Aurora borealis stones hold the colors of the rainbow. They measure 1¼". $45.00 – 65.00. (Bottom) ¾" small clip earrings are stunning. The simplicity of the two marquees with a large and small round stone amazes all. Hand set in gold-tone prongs. 1950s. $45.00 – 65.00.

6¼" earrings from the 1970s. Black tassels are topped with white marquee and chaton rhinestones. Would look great paired with a long, swan like neck. $25.00 – 45.00.

Both pair of these are from the 1980s.(Left) Original tag reads "Two Sisters," the original price tag on the back is $10.00. 2¼". $10.00 – 20.00. (Right) Pierced earrings, 1½", tag reads "Beverly Hills Elegant." $10.00 – 20.00.

All of these aurora borealis clip earrings are from the 1950s and are unsigned. Left to right: ¾", 1", ¾", 1½". All range from $40.00 – 80.00.

Left to right: Weighted multicolored clip earrings from the 1970s. The stones are glued in shallow cups. 1¼", unmarked. $30.00 – 50.00. Two-tone blue clip earrings from the 1950s. $20.00 – 30.00. Screw-on earrings, 1940s, unsigned. Blue crystal drops. Measure 1⅛". $20.00 – 30.00. These silver-tone clip earrings have large blue stones hand set in four prongs for delightful center pieces. Unsigned. ¾". $40.00 – 50.00.

(Top, left) Unmarked clip rhinestone earrings from the 1950s measure 1¼". $25.00 – 45.00. (Bottom, left) Clip earrings from the 1950s measure 1". There are marquee, pear, and two sizes of chaton stones. $30.00 – 50.00. (Top, right) Clip rhinestone earrings with large center stones are bordered by small chaton stones. 1950s. $20.00 – 40.00. (Center, right) Austrian clip earrings. Nice stars! $30.00 – 50.00. (Bottom, right) ¾" unmarked rhinestone clip earrings from the 1950s. $20.00 – 30.00.

1½" clip-on earrings are bordered with a pattern of alternating inset and outset chaton stones. Stones are hand set in silvertone prongs. Black oval center stone is 1". Unmarked. Early 1970s. $85.00 – 135.00.

(Left) Clip earrings. Two black beads/balls dangle from the dainty gold chain with prong-set faux onyx. 2¼". Unsigned. Early 1960s. $40.00 – 70.00. (Right) Clip earrings. Small rhinestones with large center stone. One braided chain with small rhinestones around the braid. 2½". Unmarked. Early 1960s. $70.00 – 100.00.

(Top) Cute clips. Silver-tone plated, set prongs. Three deep blue marquees border three aqua-colored flowers. 1". Unsigned. 1940s to 1950s. $55.00 – 75.00. (Bottom) Clip earrings. Silver-tone plating, prong set. The centers are aurora borealis stones surrounded by dark blue raised stones and other aurora borealis. Measure ¾". Unsigned. 1940s to the 1950s. $45.00 – 65.00.

(Top) Clip-on rhinestone earrings. Two marquees fringe from the round rhinestones. Very flexible. Unsigned. 1950s. $55.00 – 75.00. (Bottom) Rhinestone earrings with round, chaton-cut rhinestones. A burst of three sizes of quality stones. 1". Unsigned. 1950s. $60.00 – 80.00.

(Left) Five large pear-shaped stones with a round rhinestone for the center to bedazzle these clip-on earrings. Late 1940s to the 1950s. 1⅛". Signed "Weiss." $80.00 – 120.00. (Center) Silver-tone plated clip-on earrings that measure 1⅛". Large square, emerald, pear, and small round rhinestones make up these earrings. Signed "Weiss." Late 1940s to the 1950s. $80.00 – 120.00. (Right) Two large marquee-cut stones with smaller marquees surround a round rhinestone. Late 1940s to the 1950s. Signed "Weiss." 1¼". $80.00 – 120.00.

(Left) Signed "Lisner." Clip earrings measure 1". Mid- to late 1950s. Dress these up or down with the wardrobe! Two dark blue emerald stones with five aurora borealis rhinestones separated by three leaves and stem. $85.00 – 115.00. (Right) Clip earrings measure 1½". Hand set in prongs are the appealing blue tricolors. Blue marquees with a floral of baguettes and a faux pearl center. Each of the earrings is signed "MADE IN AUSTRIA." Early 1950s. $75.00 – 105.00.

Signed "Sarah Cov Pat Pend." Clip earrings measure 1¼". Round, open backed emerald stones embraced by silver leaves each holding a rhinestone. An overlay of two leaves covering the stone. Late 1950s to the early 1960s. $85.00 – 125.00.

(Left) These clip earrings have four marquees topped off with a round stone. Unsigned. 1¼". 1950s. $55.00 – 85.00. (Center) These clips have two thick gold ropes with dark colored aurora borealis beads in the center. Unsigned. 1950s. $40.00 – 60.00. (Right) One topaz stone is glued in the center of the five gold petals. Unsigned. 1950s. Gold tone. $30.00 – 45.00.

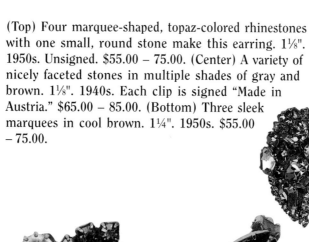

(Top) Four marquee-shaped, topaz-colored rhinestones with one small, round stone make this earring. 1⅛". 1950s. Unsigned. $55.00 – 75.00. (Center) A variety of nicely faceted stones in multiple shades of gray and brown. 1⅛". 1940s. Each clip is signed "Made in Austria." $65.00 – 85.00. (Bottom) Three sleek marquees in cool brown. 1¼". 1950s. $55.00 – 75.00.

Clip earrings signed "WEISS" measure 1½". Aurora borealis stones encompass the two royal blue marquees. A pear-shaped dark blue stone and a round stone in light aqua set off to the side. Gold tone. Stones are hand set. 1950s. $80.00 – 120.00.

(Top) 1½", 1950s clip earrings, unsigned. Three chaton topaz stones with aurora borealis bursting to the two opened back topaz stones. Unmarked. $775.00 – 795.00. (Bottom) Star clip earrings, 1", 1950s style. Round citrines with gold leaves. $70.00 – 90.00.

(Left) 1" brown plastic bead clip earrings marked "Western Germany." Early 1950s. $55.00 – 85.00. (Center) Clip earrings. Unmarked. 1". 1950s. Center of chaton topaz stones with border of delicate gold leaves. $45.00 – 55.00. (Right) Unmarked pair. Two sizes of marquees with a center aurora borealis stone. All hand set. 1¼". 1950s. $65.00 – 85.00.

Necklaces

Brazen bib. 10" bib necklace. All chaton stones are hand set in silver-tone prongs. The flexible bib has a fishhook clasp to close. The chain is adjustable. Six rows of flexible strands of rhinestones in a gradual drop. The center stones are all graduated in size. Three larger chaton stones are set on the bib's side. 1960s. Unmarked. $150.00 – 200.00.

Really ruby red! Late 1960s. Unsigned. 7" long. Stones are hand set in gold-tone prongs. Three sizes of emerald-shaped stones complete the center of this necklace. $130.00 – 170.00.

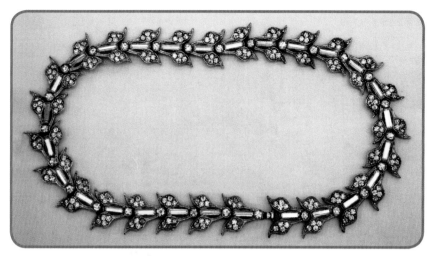

Partially platinum? No, radiantly rhodium. Weighty. This unsigned necklace is from the late 1940s to the early 1950s. Rhodium is used to achieve the platinum look. Small baguettes and small glued in rhinestones are done in the center in an alternating pattern. Each side has a leaf-like design with four small, glued-in stones. $65.00 – 95.00.

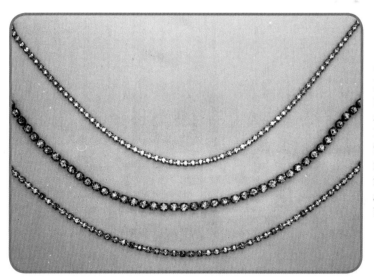

(Top) Single strand of rhinestones measuring 15". 1960s. Unsigned. Delicate stones. Silver tone. $50.00 – 70.00. (Center) 15" unsigned single strand rhinestone necklace from the 1960s. The stones are a nice size. $50.00 – 90.00. (Bottom) Single strand of rhinestones measures 16". A fishhook clasp has one small rhinestone on the tip of the hook. Small stones are hand set in the silver-tone prongs. 1960s. Unsigned. $55.00 – 75.00.

(Inner) Pretty pears! Single strand of rhinestones with fringe looped around the three pear-shaped amethyst stones. The drop matches. Stones are all hand set in the silver-tone prongs. A fishhook clasp is used to close. Unsigned. 1960s. Measures 10". $95.00 – 145.00. (Outer) 1960s. 8" silver-tone necklace is a single strand of rhinestones with a fringe of four pink stones and three dark gray marquees in a pattern of every other stone. A dark gray cabochon in a bezel setting is on each side of the necklace. A cabochon in blue, yellow, and pink makes the drop of this unusual piece. Fishhook clasp to close. All stones are hand set in the silver-tone prongs. Unsigned. $120.00 – 150.00.

13¼" necklace with the adjustable chain measuring 4". The chain is finished with a set of four tiny rhinestones that dangle from the neck. Two strands of larger rhinestones connect to the bow. All stones are hand set in the prongs. 1950s. Unsigned. $140.00 – 190.00.

(Left) I heart this piece. This single strand 8¼" rhinestone necklace is complete with the heart drop. 1960s. Unmarked. Stones are hand set in the silver-tone prongs. $50.00 – 70.00. (Center) 1950s. 8¼" rhinestone necklace has eight chaton stones attached to the sides of the single strand. The drop has four sets of four small stones with three round stones spaced between them. The clasp is finished in marciscite. Stones are all hand set in silver-tone prongs. $75.00 – 105.00. (Right) Remarkable finish! Unsigned 8" necklace. A small chaton rhinestone in a single strand with six stones on each side of the bottom of the necklace, and the drop is a larger round stone with a small chaton stone to finish. 1950s. All stones are hand set in the silver-tone prongs. $75.00 – 105.00.

(Top) This rhinestone necklace is unmarked. 3½" of rhinestones and 4" of adjustable silver-tone chain with a fishhook clasp. 1960s. Unsigned. Stones are hand set in silver-tone prongs. $45.00 – 75.00. (Bottom) Adjustable chain is 4" with a fishhook clasp. 2¾" of a single strand of rhinestones are attached to silver-tone heart shapes with four small chaton stones in a diamond shape. The drop matches the other diamond shapes. Unsigned. 1960s. $60.00 – 90.00.

(Left) Measures 7", and the adjustable chain is 3". A fishhook clasp to close complements the piece quite nicely. A simple necklace. 1950s. Unsigned. A single strand of hand-set chaton rhinestones in silver-tone prongs. The drop is two strands of rhinestones with an emerald-shaped stone in the center. $85.00 – 115.00. (Right) These stones are nice sized. They are all hand set in silver-tone prongs. Two circles of rhinestones hug the marquee center. The aqua drop is attached to two small chain links. This single strand is weighted. 1950s. Unsigned. Measures 7¾". $80.00 – 120.00.

(Left) Unsigned 1950s rhinestone necklace. Small stones in a single strand with the center drop in an aurora borealis colored, pear shape, which is bordered by two rows of very small chaton stones prong set. Silver tone. $50.00 – 70.00. (Center) Unsigned 8½" necklace. Three small stones surround the sides of the single strand. The center drop has an emerald-shaped rhinestone with three tapered baguettes that are set in silver-tone prongs. Two baguettes are topped with a single rhinestone. The center baguette is topped with two chaton stones. $45.00 – 65.00. (Right) 14" sterling chain with a marquee-shaped rhinestone drop with two rows of chaton cut stones hugging the marquee-shaped center. 1960s. $50.00 – 70.00.

(Left) 9" necklace from the 1950s. All stones are hand set in silver-tone prongs. Weighty. $80.00 – 105.00. (Right) Seven strands are set in a twist. The clasp is signed Richeliel. The beautiful clasp has pavé rhinestones set in rhodium to look like platinum with an emerald cut center stone. 1950s. 9½". $120.00 – 160.00.

A two strand rhinestone choker from the early 1960s. A fishhook clasp is used to close the 3" adjustable chain. A single rhinestone is used to finish the choker. $45.00 – 65.00.

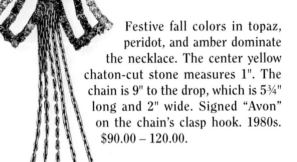

Festive fall colors in topaz, peridot, and amber dominate the necklace. The center yellow chaton-cut stone measures 1". The chain is 9" to the drop, which is 5¾" long and 2" wide. Signed "Avon" on the chain's clasp hook. 1980s. $90.00 – 120.00.

Bright belt buckle. My mimi wears this on a herringbone chain as a necklace. This weighty buckle is 3¼" long and 2" wide. ¾" yellow, oval stones with chaton-cut rhinestones make up this closed-back buckle. Late 1950s to the early 1960s. Unsigned. $180.00 – 250.00.

Vibrant necklace! This high quality necklace is comprised of round and oval stones which are all open backed. The fishhook clasp measures 5¾" and is made of oval stones with four round stones. Necklace is 14½". Unsigned. Early to mid-1950s. $125.00 – 165.00.

Fit for the neck of a princess. This silver-tone plated necklace has a fishhook clasp. A single strand of rhinestones with a drop. Three rows of rhinestones hug three marquees. On each side is an emerald center. Measures 6⅛". 1940s to the 1950s. Unsigned. $125.00 – 155.00.

This silver-tone plated necklace has round and cabochon-shaped white stones with six dark gray rhinestones raised up. An emerald cabochon sits on a silver-tone ring connecting to the center. 1940s to the 1950s. 8¾" on the left, 7" on the right. I cannot believe this is not signed! $155.00 – 210.00.

Magnificent choker that is fit for a queen. Six rows of chaton-cut rhinestones connect to five rows of chaton-cut rhinestones with a giant, gray, oval center. Total of 14½". Fishhook clasp. Unsigned. 1950s. $150.00 – 200.00.

This ultra-feminine necklace has a single strand of rhinestones with three sides of fringe dropping to showcase a magnificent center of rhinestones. Late 1940s to the early 1950s. 10". $145.00 – 200.00.

Kramer necklace which is simply elegant. A single strand of rhinestones with side fringing is simply smashing. Love the clasp which is rhodium and glued-in rhinestones. One stone is missing towards the top. Late 1940s to the mid-1950s. 11½". $120.00 – 160.00.

A single row of rhinestones flow to the drop of two rows with a fringe of baguettes and three more rows of chaton-cut rhinestones. 10⅛". Unsigned. Early 1950s to mid-1960s. $140.00 – 190.00.

Rhodium-plated necklace with a single strand of rhinestones. Three rhinestones on each side of the strand. Two large stones are on top of the three strand, flexible drop. 8¾". Signed "JEWELRY Fashions" on clasp. 1950s. $110.00 – 140.00.

Princess perfect! This 7¾" necklace has four sizes of round rhinestones with four silver bar swirls of pavé stones. Three sets of marquee and round stones on each side of the center. Fishhook clasp. Unsigned. 1940s. $115.00 – 145.00.

Signed "Coro" on the center base. This is truly great for May babies! A leaf and vine design make up this necklace. Emerald marquee and round peridot rhinestones are set in the shallow cups. Adjustable chain with a fishhook clasp. The center measures 4¾". Late 1950s to the early 1960s. $110.00 – 130.00.

I love the earthy tones of this signed Florenza necklace. Late 1950s. Seven stones in browns and greens are prong set in the center of the two peridots, three topaz stones with a drop of a small faux pearl. Adjustable chain with a fishhook clasp. The necklace measures 10¾". $120.00 – 160.00.

Pendant missing the original chain. White metal with a silver tone brushed over. Filigree in open design flows to the large center of dark blue glass. The glass is open backed. Measures 3⅛". The stone is 1¼". This antique beauty is from the late 1900s to the 1930s. $200.00 – 300.00.

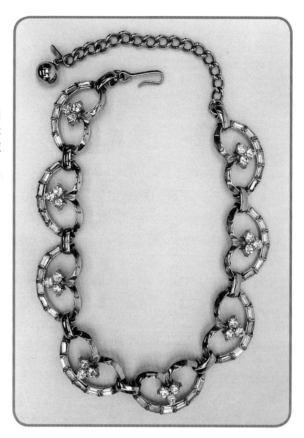

Gold-tone choker with eight hearts connected by a link. 4¼" adjustable chain with a fishhook clasp necklace that measures 11½". 1950s. Tag reads, "TARA." $105.00 – 125.00.

Sets

Demi parure. 1950s brooch is 2" and the earrings are 1". Unmarked. Gold-tone backing completes each piece. The stones are all hand set in prongs. Two colors of green with one light blue shade of stones illuminate the look. Two shapes of stones with three different sizes are used. Unsigned. For the set: $60.00 – 100.00.

Signed "Trifari." Set of clip earrings and brooch. Late 1950s. Silver-tone metal with oval shaped aqua stones. Small rhinestones are scattered throughout the pin. Brooch measures 1¾", and it is not signed, but each clip earring is. For the set: $65.00 – 95.00.

Quite the find! 7¾" necklace with a 3" adjustable chain, the fishhook clasp has 1½" of adjustable chain. Two rows of chaton stones are set in silver-tone prongs. The center drop is an open backed, tear-shaped, emerald glass stone. Nice size. The three flexible rows of rhinestones are tipped with smaller emerald tear-shaped stones. Late 1960s to the early 1970s. The matching earrings measure 2". For the set: $170.00 – 230.00.

(Outer) Eloquent emeralds. 8¼" Kramer necklace. Stones are hand set in silver-tone prongs. A larger emerald stone is separated by four smaller chaton stones. The fringe has two small, inflexible rhinestones with a larger emerald stone set on top. The center emerald stone is ¼" that falls to the oval emerald stone at ¾". Quality and weighted! Late 1960s. $200.00 – 250.00. (Inner top) 2½" unmarked, 1960s brooch. Six rows of chaton stones frame the pear-shaped emerald colored stone. $105.00 – 135.00. (Inner bottom) 1960s. Unsigned clip earrings. ¾". $45.00 – 65.00.

(Inner) With this necklace, there's always a choice of size. Adjustable chain has two small holes that you can choose for size. The adjustable chain is 2" long. The necklace measures 7". Unsigned. 1950s. White cabochons in a single strand with the four drops in a smaller size than the centers. Each has small round cabochons on top of the larger marquees. All stones are hand set in silver-tone prongs. $90.00 – 130.00. (Outer) Demi parure. The 1¼" clip earrings are signed, however, the writing is illegible. Looks like Deo? The adjustable chains measure 3" and 4½" with the necklace being 9". This set is heavy. The aurora borealis stones are set on each side of the white marquee cabochon. White enameling is over the leaves that separate the stones. Early 1950s. $90.00 – 130.00.

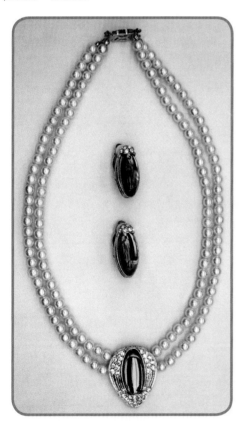

1970s demi parure. The back of the necklace clasp is stamped "M.J. 10 01." Two strands of faux pearls done in a twist with the drop of a citrine cabochon bordered by small rhinestones done on a gold-tone base. The cabochon is backed in gold-tone. 1" clip earrings. For the set: $110.00 – 150.00.

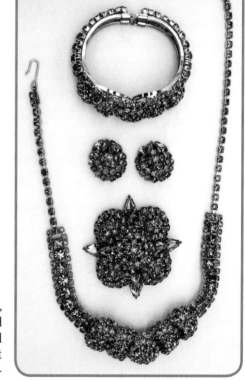

What a set! This bracelet, brooch, clip earrings, and necklace are all signed "WARNER." The bracelet is not. The brooch measures 2½", earrings are 1", the chain with the fishhook clasp measures 4", and the adjustable chain is 5½". The pink and smoky gray rhinestones contrast greatly and look splendid together. All stones are round in the necklace. The brooch and earrings are round and pear shaped. 1950s. It is getting harder and harder to find complete sets like this. For the set: $300.00 – 400.00.

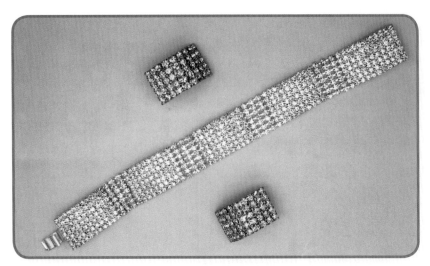

Demi parure clip earrings and bracelet, unmarked, 1970s. The earrings are 1", and the bracelet is 7⅛". Stones are set tightly together in their respective prongs. Sparkles abound! For the set: $110.00 – 140.00.

This piece gives the stars a run for their money! Demi parure. 1½" clip earrings and 7¼" necklace set. Aurora borealis stones shine. The fishhook clasp has six links in the center of the necklace, which are raised. Highly flexible. Unsigned, although it really looks like it should be. Late 1950s. For the set: $130.00 – 170.00.

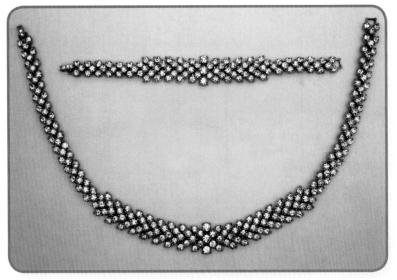

Weighty demi parure necklace that measures 15¼". The bracelet measures 7½". All the high quality chaton stones can be found in a bezel setting. 1960s, unsigned. For the set: $120.00 – 160.00.

(Top) Clip earrings are signed "Lisner." 1960s. $25.00 – 45.00. (Bottom) Bracelet with white cabochons is set on silver-tone links. 1960s. $25.00 – 45.00.

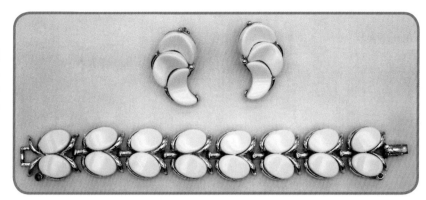

(Left) America's next big it-girl would go glam in these celeb-like pieces. Each clip earring and pin are signed "Celebrity" with the original tag from the 1970s. The tiger eye center is complemented by the gold-tone frame. $40.00 – 60.00. (Right) Each clip earring and pin are signed "Park Lane." The weighted pin converts to a brooch. $60.00 – 80.00.

(Center) Clip earrings. 3-D pair of small rhinestones in between a pair of black beads create a cross of rhinestones. Signed "Vogue." Mid- to late 1960s. $50.00 – 90.00. (Outer) Choker. Fishhook clasp with two black beads with a rhinestone spacer. 6½". Looks like Vogue. Mid- to late 1960s. $60.00 – 100.00.

Striking! Bam! This catches the eye and causes a smile. Demi-parure clip earrings and pin. Silver-tone plating, hand-set stones. All open backing. Steel blue marquees with two large emerald-shaped stones in the center and offset by 25 small aurora borealis stones. Brooch measures 3" across, earrings 1¼" long. Unmarked, a certain surprise to me. Late 1940s. For the set: $120.00 – 150.00.

An amalgam of colors! Demi-parure clip earrings and brooch. Plating is gold wash over metal, stones are set. Multi-colored cabochons and glass pieces are set on an open backing. Brooch measures 2½". Earrings are 1¼". Early 1950s. Unsigned. For the set: $110.00 – 140.00.

Pretty, precious pin and comfortable clip-on earrings. The really red round stones and aurora borealis stones are set on a gold-tone plating. The earrings match the pin with their five, small, flexible beads. 1940s to the 1950s. Each of the earrings is signed "Weiss." For the set: $120.00 – 160.00.

Demi-parure bracelet and clip earrings. Gold-tone plating. This banging bracelet has topaz-colored stones and dogtooth style set blue topaz chatons. Earrings measure 1" and the bracelet measures 6½". Late 1940s to the early 1950s. Unsigned. For the set: $95.00 – 115.00.

All pieces from the late 1940s to the 1950s. Grouping consists of all unsigned pieces. A bracelet, a set of screw-back earrings, a set of clip-on earrings, and a necklace. (Bracelet) Five rows of sparkling hand-set aquamarine chaton cut stones. Bracelet measures 5¾". $60.00 – 80.00. (Screw backs, left) Measure 1¾" with alarmingly beautiful stones. $45.00 – 50.00. (Clip earrings, right) Measure 2½" and are breath-taking. $60.00 – 65.00. (Necklace) Measures 6¾" and is made up of five rows of stones with 3¾" of a single strand to lead to a fish-hook closure. $90.00 – 120.00.

Precious pin and clip earrings set. For the pin: light yellow, citrine, and aurora borealis round stones hold three mobile fringes. The fringes are made of light yellow and aurora borealis stones. The large round stones at the top are open backed. The stones in both the earrings and the pin are set by hand on gold tone. Pin measures 2½", earrings 1". Unsigned. 1940s to the 1950s. For the set: $145.00 – 185.00.

Fantastic necklace and clip earrings. Five dark colored, topaz-shaped stones with three forming a fringe drop. The drops are surrounded by light topaz colored, chaton-cut rhinestones. One pear-shaped stone per side. A fishhook clasp is used to close. Matching clip earrings. 8" necklace, 1¼" earrings. Unsigned. Late 1940s to the mid-1950s. For the set: $185.00 – 225.00.

Elaborate necklace and screw-on earrings set. Chaton cut, topaz-colored stones with a fringe of peridot and topaz colored stones. Necklace 8½", earrings 1½". 1940s to the 1950s. Unsigned. For the set: $160.00 – 200.00.

Choker/necklace with a matching bracelet. Emeralds abound in this set. This can be a dressed up or dressed down look. Necklace measures 14¼", bracelet is 6¾". Unsigned. Late 1940s to the 1950s. For the set: $135.00 – 175.00.

Necklace and matching screw-back earrings. Two strands of chaton-cut rhinestones fade to the baguettes, then to the center which is made of two pear shapes around a central baguette at the top and bottom. A lone marquee in the middle with three square stones between the flexible fringe. 9". Unmarked. 1940s to the early 1950s. For the set: $140.00 – 190.00.

Necklace and clip earrings. A single strand cascades into two with three larger rhinestones at the end of the two strands. Four stones hold the drop of four stones and a tassel of rhinestones and pearls. Unsigned. 10½". 1940s. For the set: $130.00 – 170.00.

Parure necklace, bracelet, and clip earrings. All stones are set by hand. A marquee, then a round rhinestone series for the bracelet and necklace. Necklace has 11 stones for the adjustable clasp. Necklace is 16½", bracelet is 7½", earrings are 1¼". Necklace clasp is signed "EisenBERG," as is the bracelet clasp. Bracelet has a safety chain. For the set: $600.00 – 750.00.

Pin and screw-on earrings have aquamarine-colored stones set in unique, gold-tone displays. Unsigned. 1950s. For the set: $70.00 – 100.00.

Demi-parure star pin and clip earrings. Round and marquee stones are glued in shallow cups. Backs are open and foiled. Five marquees in the center with five on each star. A tip on the pin. A single marquee for the center attraction of the earring. Done in silver tone. 1960s. Signed "Sarah Cov" on the pin and both clip earrings. For the set: $110.00 – 140.00.

Demi-parure of clip earrings and pin done in silver tone. The pin measures 2¼" with the earrings measuring 1¾". The five tapered baguettes are hand set on each of the clip earrings. Six tapered baguettes are hand set in prongs with seven aqua rhinestones hugged with pavé aurora borealis stones. All of the baguettes are open backed. Mid- to late 1950s. Unmarked. For the set: $130.00 – 160.00.

This demi-parure is signed "Lisner" on the fishhook clasp of the necklace and each of the clip earrings. Mid- to late 1950s. Molded plastic leaves with two gold-tone leaves separated by two small aurora borealis stones on each side of the link. Necklace measures 11¼" with an adjustable chain. Earrings measure ¾". For the set: $125.00 – 155.00.

This defined brooch and clip earrings set are prong-set stones by hand. Earthy brown tones are used in the round and pear-shaped quality stones to make up the circle swirl design. Earrings measure 1⅛" and the brooch measures 2¼". Unmarked. 1940s to the early 1950s. For the set: $130.00 – 170.00.

Clip earrings and bracelet, I dare to wear. Gold-tone bracelet. Set in four prongs are eight large brown stones. Bracelet measures 7½" with the earrings measuring ¾". Unmarked. Mid-1950s. For the set: $120.00 – 160.00.

Delicate pin and clip earrings in gold tone are unsigned. The marquees are open backed on the tree of flowers. Prong-set marquees with small chaton rhinestones glued in the enameled flowers. Pin measures 3", earrings measure ¾". Early 1950s. For the set: $90.00 – 110.00.

Trifari in the original box. Set of signed pieces. This necklace is signed on the clasp and the earrings are each signed on the clip, "PAT PEND TRIFARI." Silver-tone rope chain with a fabulously designed center. Stones scream quality! Necklace measures 7⅛" with the center 2½" in width. Earrings measure 1¼". Early 1960s. For the set: $185.00 – 245.00.

Brooch and clip earrings, unsigned. The salmon-colored marquees with open back are prong set by hand. Nicely faceted stones. Six small aurora borealis stones are scattered throughout the brooch. Brooch measures 2½" with the earrings measuring 1¼". Late 1940s. For the set: $135.00 – 175.00.

Brooch is signed "BROOKCRAFT STERLING." Both earrings are signed "STERLING." 1940s. Gold wash over sterling. Stones are prong set by hand. Great design of swirls off of the fanned leaf. Emerald stones are open backed. Stones in earrings are bezel set. Brooch measures 2½" and the earrings are 1⅛". For the set: $160.00 – 200.00.

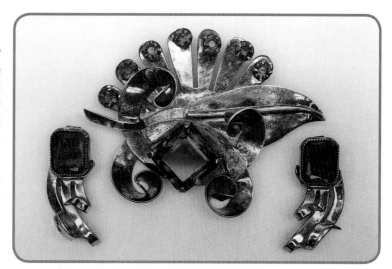

Stunning demi-parure pin and clip earrings set. Three light amethyst rhinestones are surrounded by small, dark amethysts in a circle. Five marquee-cut, aurora borealis stones are set outside the circle. A fringe of five stones, with a large center stone, completes the work. Late 1940s. Signed "Austria" on the pin and each of the clip earrings. For the set: $135.00 – 185.00.

Demi-parure clip earrings and bracelet. All stones are set by hand. Two emeralds in light yellow with topaz marquees in an every-other stone pattern. Bracelet has a safety chain. Quality! Great for a November person. Bracelet is 5¾" and the earrings are 1½". Each of the earrings and the bracelet are signed "Coro USA Pat Pending." 1940s to the 1950s. For the set: $125.00 – 165.00.

Demi-parure cuff bracelet done in mosaic. The stones are set by hand. They come in various shades of brown in pear and emerald shapes. Round topaz and red rhinestones with three small, light yellow rhinestones. Larger stones are also employed for this set. Earrings measure 1¼". 1950s. Unsigned. For the set: $190.00 – 230.00.

Demi-parure of compact and bracelet. Emerald and ruby cabochons set in heavy white enamel with rhinestones in groups of four on bracelet and compact. Compact holds the original powder puff that reads, "Evans." I don't know if this set was ever used. Compact 2½". 1950s. Unsigned, unreal. For the set: $250.00 – 350.00.

Demi-parure brooch and clip earrings set. Round and marquee faux pearls and rhinestones with a prong-set aurora borealis center stone. Done in three dimensions. 2½". Each of the clip earrings, as well as the brooch is signed, "Judy Lee." Late 1940s to the 1950s. For the set: $170.00 – 230.00.

Demi-parure pin and clip earrings set. Two rows of aurora borealis and two rows of dark pink rhinestones are varied every other row. 2¼" pin, 1⅛" earrings. 1950s. Unsigned. For the set: $130.00 – 180.00.

Screw-back earrings are each signed "STERLING." The pin is unsigned and measures 1¾". Prong-set rhinestones with open back foiled marquees for the border with round stones circling the center oval stone. 1940s. For the set: $110.00 – 160.00.

Beautiful brooch and matching clip earrings. Filigree, gold plated. Round cabochon set in the center. Seed pearls embrace the center. The eight small ruby rhinestones are bezel set. Signed "MADE IN WESTERN GERMANY" on the brooch and each of the earrings. Early 1950s. Brooch measures 2¼". Earrings are 1" long. For the set: $330.00 – 360.00.

Uptown set from the 1950s. The pin measures 2¼", screw-on earrings ¾". Six topaz marquees tip off the seven chaton rhinestones in a circle design. The center is a circle with a larger center stone. For the set: $90.00 – 120.00.

Necklace and pierced earrings from the 1950s. The necklace measures 8¾" with the earrings measuring 1¼" long. Silver tone. Stones are set by hand. Chaton rhinestones with seven royal blue emeralds topping off the five sets of flexible fringe. A fishhook clasp closes to the single royal blue rhinestone. Unsigned. For the set: $140.00 – 180.00.

A variety of colors of stones make this vivid 2½" brooch with clip earrings. Stones are set on tips of gold bars in a series of two. Center is a flower with small light citrine stones on every other flower separated by a larger stone. All stones are hand set. Unsigned. For the set: $110.00 – 140.00.

All unmarked in this set. Necklace measures 9⅛" with a ½" clasp, clip earrings 1¼", and bracelet is 7¾". 1940s. If you were born in February, this set is a perfect fit for you. For the set: $155.00 – 185.00.

Each of the earrings in this pair measures ¾" in diameter. Late 1940s to the early 1950s. Looks like Germany. $55.00 – 75.00. Pin is 1⅛" in diameter; a super star! 1940s to the early 1950s. $55.00 – 75.00.

Earrings are ¾" clips. Pear-shaped and from the 1940s. $50.00 – 80.00. Pin is a dazzling array of marquee-cut stones in a myriad of colors. $120.00 – 160.00.

(Top) Unsigned pin and clip earrings set from the 1950s. Measures 1¾" long. For the earrings: $50.00 – 90.00. For the pin: $95.00 – 125.00. (Bottom) This charming ID bracelet measures 7" and has a raised flower with eight chaton-cut rhinestones. $90.00 – 120.00.

(Center) 1⅛" ribbon pin with multicolored stones. A single blue center. 1940s. $50.00 – 70.00. (Outer) Seven gold-tone links with a single chaton stone separated by six flowers in light blue topaz with a center rhinestone. 9" adjustable staple chain with a fishhook clasp and ball. Necklace measures 8¼". Signed "Lisner." 1950s. $120.00 – 150.00.

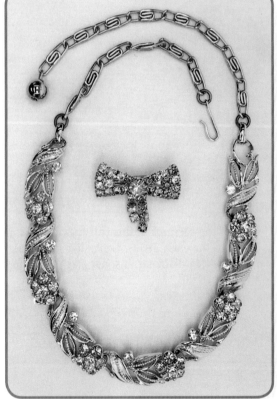

Bracelet and clip earrings. 1950s. Bracelet is 7¼". Unsigned. For the set: $120.00 – 150.00.

Ring signed "Sterling" from the mid-1950s to the early 1960s. Six small chaton rhinestones hug the right of the ocean aqua colored oval stone. Stone is nicely faceted in a four prong setting. The back is open. $130.00 – 160.00.

Miscellaneous

Nicely faceted, amber colored glass beads. Hand strung on heavy string. 11¼". 1920s. Unsigned. $155.00 – 205.00.

Going bananas! Necklace is hand strung on heavy string. 8¾" long. Unsigned. $65.00 – 105.00.

Wild about white! 11½". White glass beads with a swirl of cranberry through the white. One bead is broken. Each bead measures 1". There are 22 beads with a barrel clasp to close. Unsigned. Early 1900s to the teens. $225.00 – 265.00.

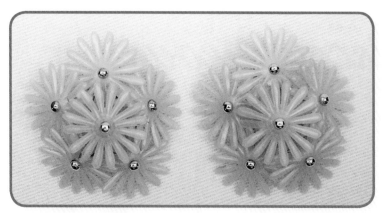

Clip-on earrings of the 1950s. These would be great with any-one's poodle skirt. Five pink plastic flowers with silver beads in the center. Unsigned. $15.00 – 25.00.

Far out feathers. Signed "JAPAN." These clip-on earrings aren't mellow yellow! Plastic feathers make up these earrings. Notice the small rhinestones on the stems. $10.00 – 20.00.

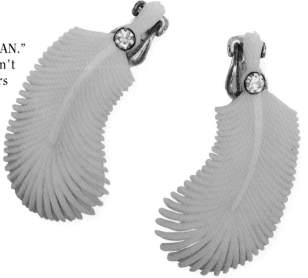

Unmarked screw-back earrings from the 1950s are done in 3-D. The white plastic flower is done in an open weave. $15.00 – 25.00.

A wonderful, bold, colorful 25" single strand of glass barrel beads strung on a fine wire. The beads are separated by six small glass beads. One blue bead is broken. Mid- to late 1900s. $180.00 – 230.00.

The 1950s were so nifty! This 17" single strand of heavy glass beads is strung tight. The beads are earthy tones and are separated by two gold-tone beads. Unsigned. $130.00 – 170.00.

Appealing colors with the faux pearls and coral-colored glass beads have great eye appeal. These are strung tight on a light string. Measures 7¾". Nice weight. Unmarked. From the late teens to the late 1920s. $95.00 – 135.00.

(Top) Early 1900s bracelet of three gold-tone links with two Persian turquoise that are open backed. 6¾". Unmarked. $110.00 – 140.00. (Bottom) Scenic bracelet is reminiscent of the 1960s. Unsigned. $125.00 – 155.00.

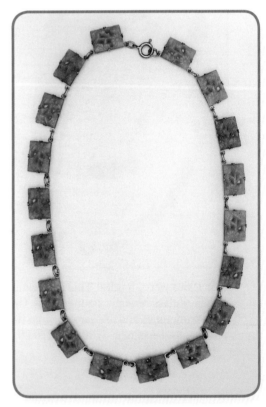

1950s dazzling 14" single strand of plastic amber beads in three shapes. Each amber bead is separated by a black plastic bead. This is strung very tight on a double string. The barrel clasp is finished in amber so as not to distract from the necklace. $90.00 – 140.00.

Necklace of "poor man's jade," commonly known as Peking glass. All are prong set by hand. Each linked by a silver ring. The back is open with a nicely detailed silver frame. Measures 7¾". Unsigned. Mid-teens to the early 1920s. $130.00 – 180.00.

Tag signed "1928," this is from the 1980s. A single strand of light blues, grays, and purples with silver metal beads to separate and a barrel clasp to close. Measures 17½". $45.00 – 85.00.

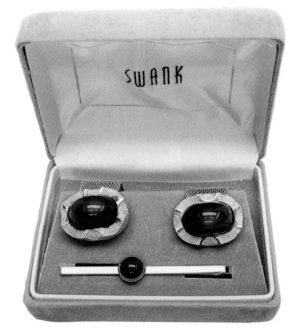

Cufflinks signed "Swank" in the original gold velvet box. Heavy gold tone with purple cabochons in the center with a matching tie clasp. 1960s to 1970s. $75.00 – 105.00.

(Top) Screw-back earrings. Mid-teens to the 1920s. Oval glass in topaz, aquamarine, and amethyst. The backs are open. Each is signed "Sterling." $60.00 – 90.00. (Bottom) Defined craftsmanship for this mid-teens to 1920s brooch. It is unsigned and weighted. A variety of colors of glass oval stones with open backs. All are prong set by hand. Silver over metal in an open filigree design. Measures 2½". $120.00 – 150.00.

Signed "Swank." Gold tone. The initial "K" done in black with a silver center background. 1960s to the 1970s. $50.00 – 90.00.

All of these are from the 1960s to the 1970s. (Left) Unmarked, round silver-tone cufflink. $20.00 – 40.00. (Center) Signed "Swank." Open gold-tone square cufflink. $18.00 – 25.00. (Right) Unmarked, gold tone, with two engraved leaves. $20.00 – 30.00.

1960s to the 1970s. Signed "PAT PEND." Weighted silver-tone frame with prong set, open backed jadite. $50.00 – 90.00.

(Left) Sterling silver oval with silver center and black flecks. 1960s to the 1970s. $50.00 – 80.00. (Center) Signed "SARAH COV.PEND." Great for a March birthday boy. 1960s to 1970s. $50.00 – 80.00. (Right) Unsigned silver-tone squares. $40.00 – 60.00.

Tie tacks. (Top) Silver tone. Signed "HICKOKUSA." Measures 1¼". 1960 to 1970. $25.00 – 45.00. (Bottom) 2¼" gold tone. Left and right side diamond design with open ends and center. 1960s to 1970. $20.00 – 30.00.

All of these are from the 1960s to 1970s. (Top) W.E.H.CO. 2¼". Initials on front of the gold-tone bar read "T E L." $30.00 – 60.00. (Center) Jaffa shrine pin. $15.00 – 25.00. (Bottom) Gold-tone bar initials are "L L." 1¼". $25.00 – 45.00.

Mint green lavaliere of the early 1900s to the late teens. 14". The pattern design is delicate. All beads are hand knotted on a heavy string. The drop string is unattached. The drop measures 3¾". Unmarked. $200.00 – 230.00.

(Top) ID Bracelet "RUTHIE 1946." The back is stamped "STERLING ROLES." $30.00 – 60.00. (Bottom) The Lord's Prayer on brass to be worn on a chain. This measures 1¼". 1940s. Perhaps this was a World War II item that saw action on faraway lands and brought home a young hero. No value assigned.

This is an adorable 23" necklace. Yellow beads separated by a small yellow bead, natural, then a yellow bead. Unsigned. Mid- to late 1900s. $170.00 – 230.00.

Each topaz-colored bead is separated by a black bead. The center stone measures 2". Late 1800s to the mid-1910s. Unsigned. $250.00 – 325.00.

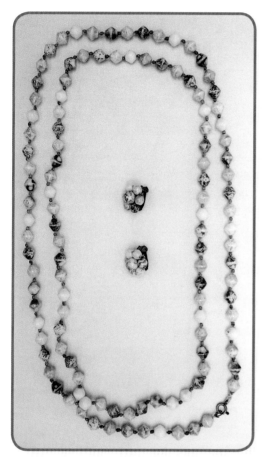

Unmarked single strand of glass beads in a variety of colors is hand strung on a heavy string. Measures 25½". The matching clip earrings are ¾". Mid- to late 1900s. $200.00 – 230.00.

Lovely, unsigned necklace from the 1920s. Necklace has 9½" chain with a 2" drop, totaling 11½". Brilliant blue glass. $180.00 – 230.00.

2½" brooch that looks like it should convert to a pendant, but does not. 1900s to the early 1920s. Unsigned. $125.00 – 155.00.

Such a delicate filigree frame for this necklace. Unsigned. Chain measures 9¾" and the stone is 1¾". $190.00 – 250.00.

Rocking ruby. The stone is set by hand. 1900s to the mid-1920s. Signed on top of the clasp, "1/20 14K." The rest is illegible. $210.00 – 290.00.

(Top) Coins are set between kinked rings. Marked "1313" on the front; stamped "II88" on the back. Measures 8½". Early 1900s. $150.00 – 200.00. (Bottom) Seven coins are connected by two sets of links. Each coin is worn in design. Late 1800s to the mid-1900s. $150.00 – 200.00.

(Top) Men's ring from the early 1930s. It is stamped "Sterling" and also "10K GOLD TOP." Nice ruby center with an open back. $130.00 – 180.00. (Bottom) Mother's ring. Seven birthstones in a range of colors. 1950s. $130.00 – 180.00.

Men's ring. Stamped "10K." Tiger's eye stone is engraved with what looks like two Greek soldiers. Early 1940s. $130.00 – 180.00.

(Left) Topical looking pin in a braided silver-tone frame. Signed "Made RM Italy." 1940s. $120.00 – 180.00. (Right) ¾" pin is a great color. Also, in great shape. Signed "Made in Italy." 1940s. $100.00 – 150.00.

Periods of Time, Styles, and Manufacturers

Art Nouveau, 1890 – 1910 — Jewelry designs are flowing, spiral, wavy, floral patterns, and a hint of nature. At this time, America is the leading industrial nation in the world. Women play the stock market and become involved in business. The bicycle becomes popular; transportation is now the automobile that only the wealthy can afford. Dancing is in vogue; records sell at a brisk pace. Jewelry is produced in America, Bohemia, Denmark, England, France, Germany, and Italy.

Art Deco, 1910 – 1930 — People are interested in the Egyptian designs, American Indians, Russian ballet, and the Paris Exposition. Stones such as lapis lazuli and carnelian are popular. Emeralds, rubies, marcasites, ivory, and Bakelite are popular for jewelry designs. In November of 1920, KDKA starts broadcasting. New magazines are being published; movies are a part of Americans' lives. The stock market soars until the great crash in 1929. Jewelry is produced in America, Bohemia, Denmark, England, France, Germany, Italy, Israel, Mexico, and South America.

In the 1920s and the 1930s, pieces marked "TFK" are produced by Trifari. The exquisite workmanship of Trifari is imitative of fine jewelry. In the 1930s and the 1940s, Trifari produces a hefty amount of rhodium-plated pieces with fine finishes. They also produce "jelly bellies," usually animal motifs whose bodies are composed of Lucite. Trifari is known for the classic crown brooch, set with cabochon stones in varied colors.

Miriam Haskell is known for a very soft design style. The pieces are hand done from beads, pearls, gilt brass, and more. In the 1930s and the 1940s, the look is beads and seed pearls. Haskell's jewelry is not signed until the end of the 1940s and the early 1950s. The Haskell company develops the antique gold finish. Miriam Haskell is active until she retires in 1950, and sells the company to her younger brother, Joe Haskell. She dies at age 82 in 1981.

In the 1930s and the 1940s, Eisenberg's jewelry is marked Eisenberg original. This company is noted for using big, bold, beautiful Austrian crystals with a great design. During the war years, many designs are in sterling and attached to or used on clothing pieces; many are made for Nordstrom's. At Christmas time, Nordstrom's is known to carry the Eisenberg Ice, consisting of top grade stones from Swarovski.

Hobé is a family of jewelers with a great history dating back 200 years. They know their customer, the woman. They want a look of antique jewelry that is affordable. From the 1930s through the 1940s, they use wonderful faceted glass stones with enamel work. In 1940, a series of floral motifs is done in sterling. Carved ivory and cinnabar are part of the Hobé design.

Art Moderne, 1935 – 1945 — Jewelry is now creative in design, losing the Nouveau style. Pieces can be brilliant to dainty looking. Three-D is in vogue. Examples of metals used in jewelry are chrome and rhodium. Women now wear designs from the Orient. Hair is worn pulled up so women can showcase their decorative earrings and necklaces. Wars are discussed. On December 7, 1941, Pearl Harbor is bombed by the Japanese, and the United States becomes involved in World War II. In 1943, a 4-4 program takes hold where teenagers can work four hours and attend school four hours per day. The war creates shortages in everything from sugar to gasoline. Americans use ration coupons. On August 14, 1945, the war ends; America celebrates everywhere with church bells ringing in communities and cities, whistles blowing, and of course, the famous kiss of the nurse and the military man. Jewelry is produced in America, Bohemia, Denmark, England, France, Germany, Italy, Israel, Mexico, and South America.

Coro, in 1946, is the largest producer of costume jewelry in America. Over 2,000 different designs are in Coro's line. Every woman can afford Coro. In 1950, a line is produced under the name Vendome.

Modern 1950s bring gold-filled, sterling, and metals used in jewelry. Due to the shortages of goods from the war, retailers and manufacturers use items that they have in inventory. Slacks and culottes are worn. In 1956, "short shorts" become the rage! Then follows the ever popular chemise. It is accessorized with costume jewelry, gloves, furs, and hats. Jewelry items include heavy beads, bibs, bracelets, and long earrings that caress the shoulder.

A

1928 Jewelry Company. 1968 to present.
Accessocraft Products Company. NY, NY 1930 – 1998, closed.
Alice Jewelry Company. Providence, RI. 1956 – 1977.
Anthony Creations, Inc. Providence, RI. 1948.
ART/MODE Art C. 1950 – 1980.
Atlas Manufacturing. NY, NY. c. 1950.
AVON. 1971 to present.

B

Bal-Ron Company, Inc. Providence, RI.
Barclay. Providence, RI. 1946.
Barrera, Jose. 1989 – 1996 designed for AVON.
Beatrix.
Beaucraft, Inc. Providence, RI. 1947 – 2004.
Bogoff. Chicago, IL. c. 1946.
Boucher. 1937 – 1970s.
BSK NY. 1948 – early 1980s.

C

Cadoro. NY, NY. 1945 – c. 1980s.
Calvaire. NY, NY. c. 1920s – 1960s.
Carnegie, Hattie. 1918 – late 1970s.
Carolee. 1972 to present.
Cassell, Burt. Providence, RI. 1953.
Cassini, Oleg. 1965.
Caviness, Alice. 1945.
Celebrity Brooklyn. NY. c. 1971.
Ciner Manufacturing. NY, NY. 1892 to present.
Coventry, Sarah. 1949 – c. 1984; 2000 to present.
Coro. NY. 1900 – 1979.

D

Danecraft. Providence, RI. 1934 to present.
DeRosa. NY, NY. 1934 – 1970.
Dior, Christian. 1948 to present.
Dodds. c. 1950. No longer in business.

E

Eisenberg. 1935 to present.

Elgin American MFG. Co. Elgin, IL. 1887.
Emmonds Jewelers, Inc. Newark, NY. 1949 – 1981.

F

Feraud, Louis.
Florenaz. 1950 – 1981.
Fred, Gary Corporation.

G

Germany
Gerry's. c. early 1950s closed in the mid 1990s.
Haskell, Miriam. 1924 to present.
Hayward. 1851 to present.
Hollywood Jewelry MFG. CO., Inc. NY. Mid 1930s to the early 1970s.

K

Karu, Kaufman, and Ruderman, Inc. NY, NY. c. 1940 – 1970s.
Kramer Jewelry Creations. NY, NY. 1943 – c. 1980.
Krementa. 1866 – 1997.

L

Laguna Royal Craftsman, Inc. NY, NY. 1944 – c. 1980s.
Lane, Kenneth J. 1963 to the present.
Lisner D. Lisner and Company of NY. 1904 to the mid 1980s.

M

Marathon Company. Alteboro, Mass. 1907 – 2005.
Marvella. NY, NY. Weinreich Brothers. 1911 to the present.
Monet Monocraft Products Company, Inc. 1927.
MUSI.

N

Napier Bliss Company. NY, NY. c. 1915 – 1999.

P

Panetta. 1945 – 1980s.
Pastelli Royal of Pittsburgh, PA. c. 1950s – 1980s.
Pell Jewelry Company. Long Island City, NY. 1941 to the present.

R

Ralph Singer Jewelry Company. 1921 to the present. ORA first used in the late 1940s.
Regency Regina Novelty Company. NY, NY. c. 1950 – 1970.
Reinad. Early 1920s – 1950s.
Renoir. 1946 – 1964.
Rosenstein, Nettie. c. 1935 – 1975.

S

Sandor. c. 1938 – 1972.
Schiaparelli. 1931 – 1973.
Schreiner. N.Y. 1939 – 1977.
Siam Silver. c. 1930s – 1980s.
Star. c. 1940s – 1960s.
Swarovski. Austria. 1895 to the present.

T

Trifari. 1918 to the present.
Tara Fifth Avenue. NYC. c. 1960s.

V

Van Dell Corporation. Providence, RI. c. 1939.
Viking Craft Albert Horwig. NY, NY.
Vogue. NYC. 1936 – mid 1970s.
Volupte – Volupte, Inc. Elizabeth, NJ.
Von Furstenberg, Diane. 1970.

W

Albert Weiss and Company, Inc. NY, NY. 1942 – 1971.
West Germany/Western Germany
Whiting, Frank M. N. Alteboro, MA. c. 1878 – c. 1960.
Whiting and Davis Plainville, MA.

XYZ

Yves St. Laurent. c. 1959.

"c." Circa within ten years before and after a date. Dates given for each mark are for when that mark was taken from. The Illusion Jewels website. For more information, please contact: jewels@illusion jewels.com or patstfy@aol.com.

Fun Facts

1896	The whistle bracelet is worn by women for protection while biking. The whistle has a two mile radius in which it can be heard.
1890 – 1920	Amber, known in Greek as "Lectron," is popular. Celluloid is now in style. It gives an expensive look.
1909	Screw-back earrings are introduced. Bracelets are worn on bare arms or over the sleeves.
1920	Pearls are the most popular necklace; a must have for any wardrobe!
1925	Long, roped beads, dangling earrings, bracelets, crystals, and rhinestones are fashionable. Birthstones are quite popular, and synthetic stones are now becoming highly advertised. Fine, faceted beads such as jet and crystal are in vogue. Belt buckles and shoe clips with rhinestones are worn.
1920 – 1930	Bakelite, a new plastic invented by Leo Hendrick Baekeland, is popular.
1933	The November 11 issue of *Collier's* magazine states that massiveness is important in jewelry. Dress, hat, fur, and handbag clips are in style.
1935	Scottie dog pins are popular and stylish.
1946	Providence, Rhode Island, is declared costume jewelry capital of the United States.
1947	Western wear clothing by Marge Riley is in vogue.
1950s	Beaded sweaters, sweater clips, rhinestones, and matching accessories are the look.
1953	Aurora borealis is new, and shoppers are drawn to the look.
1960s	Jackie O sets a fashion precedent by wearing stylish costume jewelry and clothing that are copied by women in many countries. Charm bracelets are the "it" pieces.
1970s	Women enter the workplace and are wearing real gold. Gold chains are everywhere.
1980s	These are glamorous years with the shows *Dallas*, *Dynasty*, and *Knots Landing*. The Reagans are in the White House. Barbara Bush is known for her pearls.
1990s	Women are educated about the old jewelry their grandmothers wore. They want to have the nostalgia, along with the art form, of jewelry. Interest in the "vintage market" accelerates
December 15, 2003	When asked by Diane Sawyer what he is getting Laura for Christmas, President George W. Bush's amazing response is "fake jewelry."

Glossary

Art Deco – geometrical jewelry designs of angles and lines. Originated in Paris, France. Era mid-1910s to mid-1920s.

Art Nouveau – the jewelry has curves and natural themes. Era 1895 around 1910.

Aurora Borealis – colors ranging from pale reds to yellows to a deep red color. Also known as Lumen Borealis; northern twilight popular as the northern lights. Rhinestones are treated with metals to provide the aurora color.

Baguette – a rectangular, narrow shaped stone.

Bakelite – a phenol formaldehyde resin. Bakelite was available in many colors. Bakelite was used in the production of costume jewelry, accessories, and household products.

Baroque – pearls or stones with irregular surfaces.

Base metal – a metal of a low value. Types of base metal are as follows: brass — an alloy of copper and zinc, pinch back — copper, tin, and zinc that resembles gold, white metal — has an appearance of pewter and silver, also known as pot metal.

Bezel setting – a set stone that is held securely by metal flanges embracing the stone.

Brilliant cut – stones have twice as much faceting to enhance the best sparkle of the stone.

Bugle beads – long glass tubes.

Cabochan – an unfaceted stone that is most likely round or oval and merely polished without being cut into facets.

Cap a tube or cone-shape cup – closed at one end, holds a bead or pearl.

Carnelian (cornelian) – a translucent, dull red quartz with a waxy finish, often used in Art Deco jewelry, seals, and intaglios.

Casting jewelry – often formed by a lost wax method, pouring a metal into a mold, usually rubber, that makes an impression when it hardens, producing a piece with weight and depth.

Channel (Cha-nel) setting – rhinestones are placed in a channel cut into the metal with the top edge of the channel bent over the stones to retain them.

Charms – objects worn initially for their protective properties, attracting good luck or averting ill health, now worn to commemorate an event or as a fashion object.

Chatelaine – formerly used to describe a chain attached to an ornamental brooch or hook worn at the waist, from which was suspended various objects used by the wearer. Examples: keys, watches, or purses.

Chaton – a popular cut in round stones found in costume jewelry.

Choker – a short necklace around 15" long worn high on the neck. Popular in the 1950s, a major fashion comeback in the 1970s.

Celluloid – an early plastic that was used in hair accessories, dresser sets, and costume jewelry.

Chromium – a shiny, hard, and brittle metal. A grayish white metallic that does not rust easily.

Cloisonne (cloy-sa-nay) – enamel divided by sections of metal on a metal base.

Cut beads – faceted glass beads that reflect, glitter, and sparkle.

Die-stamping – dies are created from models made according to designers' drawings, then machines stamp out stampings of brass, sterling silver, or other metals. They are then trimmed, soldered, polished, plated, and lacquered.

Dog collar – popular in the 1960s. A broad necklace worn tightly around the neck.

Electroplate – process of fusing metals of different qualities.

Enamel – process of melting a glasslike substance and then cooling it to make a smooth hard surface, painting and varnishing the smooth surface in costume jewelry.

Emerald cut – a square cut stone.

Fancy cut – stones in unusual shapes. Example: hearts, half moons.

Faux – not genuine; fake or false.

Filigree – a decorative pattern made of wires and done in open work.

Filigree – twisted and soldered fine strands of wire in intricate, lacy patterns.

Findings – functional parts of jewelry. Closing used to close a piece of jewelry: clasp, hooks, and rings. Fastenings used to hold jewelry to clothing or to the body: clips, clutches, and pins. Joinings hold parts of jewelry together: bezels, colts, caps, cords, chains, head and eye pins; loops and wires.

Foiled – stone silver or gold metallic foil that is behind the stone. Enhances the glitz.

French jet – black cabochon cut stone used in the Victorian era (1837 – 1901). Light in weight, and they really sparkle.

Gilding – an application of gold onto a surface of another object produced from another material.

Gold filled – two thin slices of gold with another metal in between. Jewelry is marked with the carat weight of gold content and the initials "g.f."

Graduated – necklace strung with larger stones in the front, which taper to smaller stones towards the back.

Hand set – stones that are placed individually in the metal setting.

Hematite (He-ma-tite) – blue/black stones used for intaglio and beads.

Intaglio (In-ta-glio) – engraving cut into a stone; if the stone is pressed into a softer material, an image is produced in relief.

Japanned – a process which colors metals to a dull black.

Jet – coal with a high polish used in jewelry.

Juliana jewelry – a style of jewelry. Quality abounds with colorful stones and showcase designs. Well manufactured, weighty, and well constructed. Collectible and sought after. William DeLizza, a founder of DeLizza and Elster factory (D @ E), named the jewelry after his mom, Juliana.

Lapis lazuli (La-zu-li) – opaque silicate; dark blue with white dots, often simulated for costume jewelry.

Lobster claw clasp – clasp or closure shaped like a "lobster's claw." Easy open and close.

Lavalliere – a thin chain with a single suspended drop or stone. May be spelled lavaliere.

Lucite – patented in 1941 by the Dupont Company. Types of transparent plastics.

Marcasite – metallic faceted stones made from iron pyrite.

Marked – when a manufacturer's or designer's identifying mark is stamped, carved, or signed into the jewelry.

Moonstone – bluish translucent stone; used in jewelry in the 1930s and 1940s, often simulated.

Parcel-gilt – silver objects which have been somewhat enriched with gilding.

Parure – set of matched jewelry.

Paste – imitation rhinestones or diamonds.

Patina – a green rust that occurs on jewelry and other metals when they hold a high bronze or copper content.

Pavé – setting of stones placed together closely so no metal is showing.

Pear cut – cut in the shape of a tear or a pear.

Pendant – movable ornament suspended from a chain or another part of the ornament.

Prystal – plastic substitute imitating glass.

Retro – back, behind, and prior. Already used in the past and will be used in the future.

Rhinestone – an imitation diamond, made of glass.

Rhodium – an extremely hard and brittle metal with a white color and a metallic luster. Looks like platinum. Discovered in 1803 among grains of crude platinum.

Rondelle – these are used as spacers in strands of beads and pearls. Two metal discs with small rhinestones set in between.

Scatter pins – small pins. Usually butterflies, birds, insects, or flowers. Worn in groups. Popular in the 1950s.

Signed – when a manufacturer's or designer's identifying mark or signature is etched, carved, or stamped into the jewelry.

Tapered baguettes – narrow, rectangular shape that is large at one end and tapers downward to a smaller size.

Unsigned or unmarked – jewelry that was not stamped, carved, or etched by the designer or manufacturer.

White metal – a mix of zinc, lead, and tin with cadmium.

Zircon – silicate of zirconium; transparent crystals in various colors.

Bibliography

Aswad & Weinstein. *The Art & Mystique of Shell Cameos.* Florence, AL: Books Americana, 1991.

Avon pamphlet, c 1993. Avon Products, Inc.

Baker, Lillian. *Art Nouveau & Art Deco Jewelry, An Identification & Value Guide.* Paducah, KY: Collector Books, 1981.

_____. *Fifty Years of Collectible Fashion Jewelry, 1925 – 1975.* Paducah, KY: Collector Books, 1986.

_____. *100 Years of Collectible Jewelry, An Identification and Value Guide.* Paducah, KY: Collector Books, 1978.

Bell, Jeanenne. *Answers to Questions About Old Jewelry 1840 – 1950, 2nd Edition.* Florence, AL: Books Americana, 1985.

Brown, Marcia. *Signed Beauties of Costume Jewelry, Volume II, Identification and Values.* Paducah, KY: Collector Books, 2004.

_____. *Unsigned Beauties of Costume Jewelry, Identification and Values.* Paducah, KY: Collector Books, 2000.

Bruton, LaRee Johnson. *Ladies Vintage Accessories Identification and Value Guide.* Paducah, KY: Collector Books, 2001.

Dolan, Maryanne. *Collecting Rhinestone Colored Jewelry, An Identification & Value Guide, 2nd Edition.* Florence, AL: Books Americana, 1989.

_____. *Collecting Rhinestone and Colored Jewelry, An Identification & Value Guide, 3rd Edition.* Florence, AL: Books Americana, 1993.

Edeen, Karen L. *Vintage Jewelry for Investment and Casual Wear.* Paducah, KY: Collector Books, 2002.

Gallina, Jill. *Christmas Pins Past and Present, Second Edition.* Paducah, KY: Collector Books, 2004.

Henzel, Sylvia S. *Collectible Costume Jewelry, Revised Edition.* Radnor, PA: Wallace-Homestead, 1987.

_____. *Collectible Costume Jewelry Id & Value Guide, 3rd Edition.* Iola, WI: Krause Publications, 1997.

Kaplan, Arthur Guy. *Offical Price Guide to Antique Jewelry.* New York, NY: Random House, 1990.

Leshner, Leigh. *Rhinestone Jewelry, A Price and Identification Guide.* Iola, WI: Krause Publications, 2003.

_____. *Vintage Jewelry, A Price Guide and Identification Guide, 1920s – 1940s.* Iola, WI: Krause Publications, 2002.

Marsh, Madeleine. *Miller's Collectibles Price Guide.* Heron Quay's, London: Octopus Publishing Group LTD. 1999.

Miller, Harrice Simmons. *Costume Jewelry Official Identification & Price Guide, First Edition.* New York, NY: Random House, 1990.

_____. *Costume Jewelry, The Confident Collector, 2nd Edition.* New York, NY: Avon, 1994.

Remero, Christie. *Warman's Jewelry Encyclopedia of Antique and Collectibles.* Radnor, PA: Wallace-Homestead Book Company, 1995.

Rivers, Joan. *Jewelry by Joan Rivers.* New York, NY: Abbeyville Press, 1995.

Schiffer, Nancy and Lyngerda Kelly. *Costume Jewelry, the Great Pretenders Revised, 4th Edition.* Atglen, PA: 2002.

Simonds, Cherri. *Collectible Costume Jewelry.* Paducah, KY: Collector Books, 1997.

Smith, Pamela. *Price Guide to Vintage Fashion and Fabrics.* New York, New York: House of Collectibles, 2001.

Snell, Doris J. *Antique Jewelry with Prices.* Radnor, PA: Wallace-Homestead Book Company, 1984.

Tait, Hugh. *Jewelry, 7,000 Years.* New York, NY: Harry N. Abrams, Incorporated, 1987.

TWO MORE Charming Books by Ronna Lee Aikins

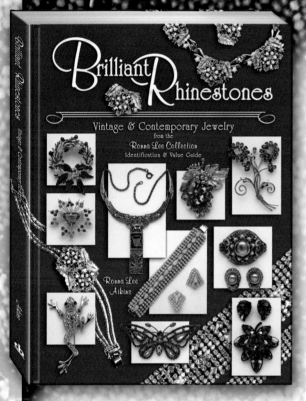

BRILLIANT RHINESTONES

With over 750 sparkling color photos identifying over 950 pieces, the beauty of this book will be evident. Some of the designers featured include Coro, Lisner, Kramer, Haskell, Trifari, Judy Lee, Hattie Carnegie, Napier, Beau Jewels, and Gerry's. There is also a West Germany and Austrian chapter, and a special dealers' directory that includes 100 organizations and their contact information. Brilliant Rhinestones helps you consider the design of the piece when selecting an item for your collection, and gives you "the eye to buy." There are also 25 vintage advertisements that showcase the costume jewelry of the past, as well as signed sterling from the 1960s and 1970s, men's pieces, and other fun accessories.

Item #6122 · 8½ x 11 · 224 Pgs. · HB · $24.95

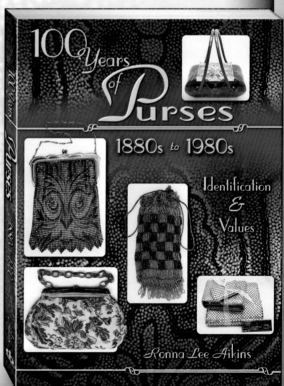

100 YEARS OF PURSES, 1880s to 1980s

This book will identify, by chapter, purse styles over a 100-year span, from 1880 to 1980. Any female who loves or is fascinated with handbags must own this book. More than 320 photos showcase creative, stylish, flamboyant, prestigious, and conventional purses. You will learn that the handbag creates a mystery about the owner. Discussed are purses of all types: beaded, evening, Lucite, pearl, straw, reptile, tapestry, and bags from the 1940s to the 1960s. There is also a chapter on German silver, compacts, and accessories. This book is truly a delight for purse lovers of all ages.

Item #6645 · 8½ x 11 · 144 Pgs. · PB · $24.95

ORDER YOURS TODAY!

www.collectorbooks.com

Collector Books · 5801 Kentucky Dam Road · P. O. Box 3009 · Paducah, KY 42003-3009 · TOLL FREE 1-800-626-5420

© Collector Books 2008

more great TITLES from collector books

DOLLS

6315 **American Character Dolls**, Izen $24.95
7346 **Barbie Doll** Around the World, 1964 – 2007, Augustyniak.....................$29.95
2079 **Barbie Doll** Fashion, Volume I, Eames $24.95
6319 **Barbie Doll** Fashion, Volume III, Eames $29.95
7621 Collectible African American Dolls, Ellis..............$29.95
6546 Collector's Ency. of **Barbie** Doll Exclusives & More, 3rd Ed., Augustyniak $29.95
6920 Collector's Encyclopedia of American **Composition Dolls**, Volume I, Mertz.....$29.95
6451 Collector's Encyclopedia of American **Composition Dolls**, Volume II, Mertz...$29.95
6636 Collector's Encyclopedia of **Madame Alexander Dolls**, Crowsey $24.95
6456 Collector's Guide to **Dolls of the 1960s and 1970s**, Volume II, Sabulis ...$24.95
6944 The Complete Guide to **Shirley Temple** Dolls and Collectibles, Bervaldi-Camaratta $29.95
7028 **Doll Values**, Antique to Modern, 9th Edition, Edward.........$14.95
7634 Madame Alexander 2008 Collector's Dolls Price Guide #33, Crowsey $14.95
6467 **Paper Dolls** of the 1960s, 1970s, and 1980s, Nichols.........$24.95
6642 20th Century **Paper Dolls**, Young.........$19.95

TOYS

6938 Everett Grist's Big Book of **Marbles**, 3rd Edition $24.95
7523 **Breyer Animal** Collector's Gde., 5th Ed., Browell/Korber-Weimer/Kesicki....$24.95
7527 Collecting Disneyana, Longest $29.95
7356 Collector's Guide to Housekeeping Toys, Wright $16.95
7528 Collector's Toy Yearbook, 100 Years of Great Toys, Longest.....................$29.95
7355 **Hot Wheels**, The Ultimate Redline Guide Companion, Clark/Wicker $29.95
7635 **Matchbox Toys**, 1947 to 2007, 5th Edition, Johnson.........$24.95
7539 **Schroeder's Collectible Toys**, Antique to Modern Price Guide, 11th Ed. $19.95
6650 **Toy Car** Collector's Guide, 2nd Edition, Johnson $24.95

JEWELRY, WATCHES & PURSES

4704 Antique & Collectible **Buttons**, Wisniewski $19.95
4850 Collectible **Costume Jewelry**, Simonds $24.95
5675 Collectible **Silver Jewelry**, Rezazadeh $24.95
6468 Collector's Ency. of Pocket & Pendant **Watches**, 1500 – 1950, Bell $24.95
6554 **Coro Jewelry**, Brown $29.95
7529 **Costume Jewelry 101**, 2nd Edition, Carroll..............$24.95
7025 **Costume Jewelry 202**, Carroll..............$24.95
4940 **Costume Jewelry**, A Practical Handbook & Value Guide, Rezazadeh $24.95
5812 Fifty Years of Collectible **Fashion Jewelry**, 1925 – 1975, Baker $24.95
6833 **Handkerchiefs**: A Collector's Guide, Volume II, Guarnaccia/Guggenheim $24.95
6464 Inside the **Jewelry** Box, Pitman..............$24.95
7358 Inside the **Jewelry** Box, Volume 2, Pitman $24.95
5695 **Ladies' Vintage Accessories**, Johnson $24.95
1181 100 Years of Collectible **Jewelry**, 1850 – 1950, Baker $9.95
6645 100 Years of **Purses**, 1880s to 1980s, Aikins $24.95
7626 Pictorial Guide to Costume Jewelry, Bloom..............$29.95
6942 **Rhinestone Jewelry**: Figurals, Animals, and Whimsicals, Brown $24.95

ARTIFACTS, GUNS, KNIVES, & TOOLS

6039 Signed Beauties of **Costume Jewelry**, Brown $24.95
6341 Signed Beauties of **Costume Jewelry**, Volume II, Brown $24.95
7625 20th Century **Costume Jewelry**, 2nd Edition, Aikins $24.95
5620 Unsigned Beauties of **Costume Jewelry**, Brown $24.95

1868 Antique **Tools**, Our American Heritage, McNerney $9.95
6822 **Antler, Bone & Shell** Artifacts, Hothem...........$24.95
1426 **Arrowheads & Projectile Points**, Hothem...........$7.95
6231 **Indian Artifacts** of the Midwest, Book V, Hothem...........$24.95
7037 **Modern Guns**, Identification & Values, 16th Ed., Quertermous $16.95
7034 **Ornamental Indian Artifacts**, Hothem $34.95
6567 **Paleo-Indian Artifacts**, Hothem...........$29.95
6569 **Remington Knives**, Past & Present, Stewart/Ritchie $16.95
7366 Standard Guide to **Razors**, 3rd Edition, Stewart/Ritchie...........$12.95
7035 Standard **Knife** Collector's Guide, 5th Edition, Ritchie/Stewart $16.95

PAPER COLLECTIBLES & BOOKS

6623 Collecting **American Paintings**, James...........$29.95
7039 Collecting **Playing Cards**, Pickvet $24.95
6826 Collecting Vintage **Children's Greeting Cards**, McPherson...........$24.95
6553 Collector's Guide to **Cookbooks**, Daniels $24.95
1441 Collector's Guide to **Post Cards**, Wood $9.95
7622 Encyclopedia of Collectible Children's Books, Jones...........$29.95
7636 The Golden Age of Postcards, Early 1900s, Penniston...........$24.95
6936 **Leather Bound Books**, Boutiette $24.95
7036 **Old Magazine Advertisements**, 1890 – 1950, Clear $24.95
6940 **Old Magazines**, 2nd Edition, Clear...........$19.95
3973 **Sheet Music** Reference & Price Guide, 2nd Ed., Pafik/Guiheen $19.95
6837 Vintage **Postcards** for the Holidays, 2nd Edition, Reed...........$24.95

GLASSWARE

7362 American Pattern Glass Table Sets, Florence/Cornelius/Jones...........$24.95
6930 Anchor Hocking's **Fire-King** & More, 3rd Ed., Florence $24.95
7524 Coll. **Glassware** from the 40s, 50s & 60s, 9th Edition, Florence $19.95
6921 Collector's Encyclopedia of **American Art Glass**, 2nd Edition, Shuman $29.95
7526 Collector's Encyclopedia of **Depression Glass**, 18th Ed., Florence $19.95
3905 Collector's Encyclopedia of **Milk Glass**, Newbound $24.95
7026 Colors in **Cambridge Glass** II, Natl. Cambridge Collectors, Inc...........$29.95
7029 **Elegant Glassware** of the Depression Era, 12th Edition, Florence $24.95
6334 Encyclopedia of **Paden City Glass**, Domitz $29.95
3981 Evers' Standard **Cut Glass** Value Guide $12.95
6126 **Fenton Art Glass**, 1907 – 1939, 2nd Ed., Whitmyer...........$29.95
6628 **Fenton Glass** Made for Other Companies, Domitz...........$29.95
7030 **Fenton Glass** Made for Other Companies, Volume II, Domitz...........$29.95
6462 Florences' **Glass Kitchen Shakers**, 1930 – 1950s $19.95

1.800.626.5420 Mon. – Fri. 7 am – 5 pm CT   Fax: 1.270.898.8890

5042 Florences' **Glassware Pattern Identification** Guide, Vol. I $18.95
5615 Florences' **Glassware Pattern Identification** Guide, Vol. II $19.95
6643 Florences' **Glassware Pattern Identification** Guide, Vol. IV $19.95
6641 Florences' **Ovenware** from the 1920s to the Present $24.95
7630 **Fostoria** Stemware, The Crystal for America, 2nd Edition, Long/Seate $29.95
6226 **Fostoria** Value Guide, Long/Seate $19.95
6127 The **Glass Candlestick** Book, Volume 1, Akro Agate to Fenton, Felt/Stoer $24.95
6228 The **Glass Candlestick** Book, Volume 2, Fostoria to Jefferson, Felt/Stoer $24.95
6461 The **Glass Candlestick** Book, Volume 3, Kanawha to Wright, Felt/Stoer $29.95
6648 Glass **Toothpick Holders**, 2nd Edition, Bredehoft/Sanford.........$29.95
5827 **Kitchen Glassware** of the Depression Years, 6th Edition, Florence $24.95
7534 **Lancaster Glass** Company, 1908–1937, Zastowney $29.95
7359 **L.E. Smith Glass** Company, Felt $29.95
6133 **Mt. Washington Art Glass**, Sisk $49.95
7027 Pocket Guide to **Depression Glass** & More, 15th Edition, Florence $12.95
7623 Standard Encyclopedia of **Carnival Glass**, 11th Ed., Carwile $29.95
7624 Standard **Carnival Glass** Price Guide, 16th Ed., Carwile $9.95
6566 Standard Encyclopedia of **Opalescent Glass**, 5th Ed., Edwards/Carwile $29.95
7364 Standard Encyclopedia of **Pressed Glass**, 5th Ed., Edwards/Carwile $29.95
6476 **Westmoreland Glass**, The Popular Years, 1940–1985, Kovar $29.95

POTTERY

6922 **American Art Pottery**, 2nd Edition, Sigafoose $24.95
6326 Collectible **Cups & Saucers**, Book III, Harran $24.95
6331 Collecting **Head Vases**, Barron $24.95
6943 Collecting **Royal Copley**, Devine.........$19.95
6621 Collector's Encyclopedia of **American Dinnerware**, 2nd Ed., Cunningham ...$29.95
5034 Collector's Encyclopedia of **California Pottery**, 2nd Ed., Chipman $24.95
6629 Collector's Encyclopedia of **Fiesta**, 10th Ed., Huxford.........$24.95
1276 Collector's Encyclopedia of **Hull Pottery**, Roberts $19.95
5609 Collector's Encyclopedia of **Limoges Porcelain**, 3rd Ed., Gaston $29.95
6637 Collector's Encyclopedia of **Made in Japan Ceramics**, First Ed., White $24.95
5841 Collector's Encyclopedia of **Roseville Pottery**, Vol. 1, Huxford/Nickel $24.95
5842 Collector's Encyclopedia of **Roseville Pottery**, Vol. 2, Huxford/Nickel.........$24.95
6646 Collector's Ency. of **Stangl Artware, Lamps, and Birds**, 2nd Ed., Runge $29.95
6634 Collector's Ultimate Ency. of **Hull Pottery**, Volume 1, Roberts.........$29.95
6829 The Complete Guide to **Corning Ware & Visions Cookware**, Coroneos.........$19.95
7530 Decorative **Plates**, Harran $29.95
7638 Encyclopedia of Universal Potteries, Chorey $29.95
7628 English China Patterns & Pieces, Gaston $29.95
5918 Florences' Big Book of **Salt & Pepper Shakers** $24.95
6320 Gaston's **Blue Willow**, 3rd Edition $19.95
6630 Gaston's **Flow Blue China**, The Comprehensive Guide.........$29.95
7021 Hansons' American **Art Pottery** Collection.........$29.95
7032 **Head Vases**, 2nd Edition, Cole.........$24.95
2379 Lehner's Ency. of **U.S. Marks** on Pottery, Porcelain & China, no values $24.95
4722 **McCoy Pottery** Collector's Reference & Value Guide, Hanson/Nissen $19.95

5913 **McCoy Pottery**, Volume III, Hanson/Nissen $24.95
6835 **Meissen** Porcelain, Harran $29.95
7536 The Official **Precious Moments**® Collector's Guide to **Figurines**, 3rd Ed., Bomm ...$19.95
6335 Pictorial Guide to **Pottery & Porcelain Marks**, Lage, No values $29.95
1440 **Red Wing Stoneware**, DePasquale/Peck/Peterson $9.95
6838 **R.S. Prussia** & More, McCaslin $29.95
7637 **RumRill Pottery**, The Ohio Years, 1938–1942, Fisher.........$29.95
6945 **TV Lamps** to Light the World, Shuman $29.95
7043 **Uhl Pottery**, 2nd Edition, Feldmeyer/Holtzman $16.95
6828 The Ultimate Collector's Encyclopedia of **Cookie Jars**, Roerig $29.95
6640 Van Patten's ABC's of Collecting **Nippon Porcelain** $29.95

OTHER COLLECTIBLES

7627 Antique and Collectible Dictionary, Reed, No values $24.95
6446 Antique & Contemporary **Advertising Memorabilia**, 2nd Edition, Summers $29.95
6935 Antique **Golf Collectibles**, Georgiady.........$29.95
1880 Antique **Iron**, McNerney $9.95
7024 B.J. Summers' Guide to **Coca-Cola**, 6th Edition $29.95
1128 **Bottle** Pricing Guide, 3rd Ed., Cleveland $7.95
7532 Bud Hastin's **Avon** Collector's Encyclopedia, 18th Edition.........$29.95
6924 Captain John's **Fishing Tackle** Price Guide, 2nd Edition, Kolbeck $24.95
6342 Collectible **Soda Pop** Memorabilia, Summers $24.95
6625 Collector's Encyclopedia of **Bookends**, Kuritzky/De Costa $29.95
7365 Collector's Guide to Antique **Radios**, 7th Edition, Slusser/Radio Daze.........$24.95
7023 The Complete Guide to Vintage **Children's Records**, Muldavin $24.95
6928 Early **American Furniture**, Obbard $19.95
7042 The Ency. of Early American & Antique **Sewing Machines**, 3rd Ed., Bays $29.95
7031 **Fishing Lure** Collectibles, An Ency. of the Early Years, Murphy/Edmisten $29.95
7629 **Flea Market Trader**, 17th Edition $15.95
6458 **Fountain Pens**, Past & Present, 2nd Edition, Erano $24.95
7631 **Garage Sale** & Flea Market Annual, 16th Edition $19.95
3906 **Heywood-Wakefield** Modern Furniture, Rouland $18.95
7033 Hot **Kitchen & Home** Collectibles of the 30s, 40s, and 50s, Zweig.........$24.95
7038 The Marketplace Guide to **Oak Furniture**, 2nd Edition, Blundell $29.95
6939 Modern Collectible **Tins**, 2nd Edition, McPherson.........$24.95
6564 Modern **Fishing Lure** Collectibles, Volume 3, Lewis $24.95
6832 Modern **Fishing Lure** Collectibles, Volume 4, Lewis $24.95
7349 Modern **Fishing Lure** Collectibles, Volume 5, Lewis $29.95
6322 Pictorial Guide to **Christmas Ornaments** & Collectibles, Johnson $29.95
6842 Raycrafts' **Americana** Price Guide & DVD $19.95
6923 Raycrafts' **Auction Field Guide**, Volume One, Price Guide & DVD.........$19.95
7538 **Schroeder's Antiques** Price Guide, 26th Edition $17.95
6038 **Sewing Tools** & Trinkets, Volume 2, Thompson $24.95
5007 **Silverplated Flatware**, Revised 4th Edition, Hagan $18.95
7367 **Star Wars** Super Collector's Wish Book, 4th Edition, Carlton $29.95
7537 Summers' Pocket Guide to **Coca-Cola**, 6th Edition $14.95
6841 Vintage **Fabrics**, Gridley/Kiplinger/McClure $19.95

This is only a partial listing of the books on antiques that are available from Collector Books. All books are well illustrated and contain current values. Most of these books are available from your local bookseller, antique dealer, or public library. If you are unable to locate certain titles in your area, you may order by mail from COLLECTOR BOOKS, P.O. Box 3009, Paducah, KY 42002-3009. Customers with Visa, MasterCard, or Discover may place orders by fax, by phone, or online. Add $5.00 postage for the first book ordered and 60¢ for each additional book. Include item number, title, and price when ordering. Allow 14 to 21 days for delivery.

| News for Collectors | Request a Catalog | Meet the Authors | Find Newest Releases | Calendar of Events | Special Sale Items |

www.collectorbooks.com

Schroeder's
ANTIQUES
Price Guide

OUR #1 BEST-SELLER!

FULL COLOR!

#1 BESTSELLING
ANTIQUES PRICE GUIDE

≈ Almost 40,000 listings in hundreds of categories
≈ Histories and background information
≈ Both common and rare antiques featured

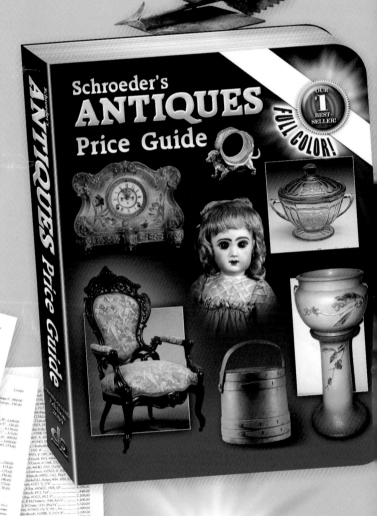

only
$19.95
608 pages

COLLECTOR BOOKS
P.O. BOX 3009, Paducah KY, 42002-3009

1.800.626.5420

www.collectorbooks.com